AUSTIN
Food Crawls

Kelsey Kennedy

TOURING *the* NEIGHBORHOODS
ONE BITE & LIBATION *at a* TIME

Globe
Pequot
GUILFORD, CONNECTICUT

Globe
Pequot

An imprint of The Rowman & Littlefield Publishing Group, Inc.
4501 Forbes Blvd., Ste. 200
Lanham, MD 20706
www.rowman.com

Distributed by NATIONAL BOOK NETWORK

Maps by Melissa Baker

British Library Cataloguing in Publication Information available

Library of Congress Cataloging-in-Publication Data available

ISBN 978-1-4930-4146-6 (paperback)
ISBN 978-1-4930-4147-3 (e-book)

∞™ The paper used in this publication meets the minimum requirements of American National Standard for Information Sciences—Permanence of Paper for Printed Library Materials, ANSI/NISO Z39.48-1992,

Printed in the United States of America

Contents

Introduction

WELCOME TO AUSTIN!

This city is on every foodie's bucket list, and for good reason: It's where you'll find some of the best barbecue joints in the world, a slew of award-winning breweries, and a rapidly growing scene of gorgeous farm-to-table restaurants. Breakfast tacos are practically a religion here, and hundreds of food trucks offer everything from Detroit-style pizza to Italian gelato to Mexican street tacos. The mild Austin winters mean that you can enjoy wine gardens, rooftop bars, and outdoor patios year-round. No matter what lifestyle or diet you follow, Austin is a foodie's playground.

Austin has been growing faster than it can handle. It's bursting at the seams with people and traffic and noise, and a lot of folks complain about that. But I don't mind the crowds too much, because every person who moves to Austin brings new energy and ideas, which might eventually lead to the next great fusion-fare food truck, new-school BBQ joint, or craft cocktail bar. Austin is full of so much life, food, and fun, and I'm glad y'all are here.

Follow the Icons

 If you eat something outrageous and don't take a photo for Instagram, did you really eat it? These restaurants feature dishes that are Instagram famous. The foods must be seen (and snapped) to be believed, and luckily they taste as good as they look!

 Cheers to a fabulous night out in Austin! These spots add a little glam to your grub and are perfect for marking a special occasion.

 Follow this icon when you're crawling for cocktails. This symbol points out the establishments that are best known for their great drinks. The food never fails here, but be sure to come thirsty, too!

 This icon means that sweet treats are ahead. Bring your sweet tooth to these spots for dessert first (or second or third).

 Austin is for brunch. Look for this icon when crawling with a crew that needs sweet and savory (or an excuse to drink before noon).

THE BOULDIN CREEK CRAWL

1. Start your morning with a homemade vegetarian breakfast at **BOULDIN CREEK CAFE**, 1900 S. 1ST ST., AUSTIN, (512) 416-1601, BOULDINCREEKCAFE.COM

2. Grab a pint at America's favorite brewpub, **THE AUSTIN BEER GARDEN BREWING COMPANY**, 1305 W. OLTORF ST., AUSTIN, (512) 298-2242, WWW .THEABGB.COM

3. Cozy up next to your date at **LENOIR**, 1807 S. 1ST ST., AUSTIN, (512) 215-9778, LENOIRRESTAURANT.COM

4. Indulge in award-winning cupcakes at **SUGAR MAMA'S BAKESHOP**, 1905 S. 1ST ST., AUSTIN, (512) 448-3727, SUGARMAMASBAKESHOP.COM

5. Celebrate someone special at **MATTIE'S AT GREEN PASTURES**, 811 W. LIVE OAK ST., AUSTIN, (512) 444-188, MATTIESAUSTIN.COM

6. End your night with a scoop of authentic Italian gelato at **DOLCE NEVE GELATO**, 1713 S. 1ST ST., AUSTIN, (512) 804-5568, DOLCENEVEGELATO .COM

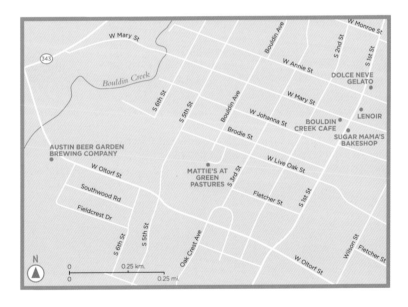

Bouldin Creek

Keeping the "Hip" in Hippie

BOULDIN CREEK IS FUNKY, QUIRKY, AND CONSTANTLY EVOLVING. When folks think "Austin, Texas," this neighborhood is often what they envision: old Mexican bakeries next to grungy tattoo parlors, hip little wine bars with sprawling patios decked out with twinkly lights, hodgepodge streets of houses with both 1950s bungalows and modern rebuilds, decades-old graffiti, small sidewalks shaded by live oak trees, and cashonly food trucks with lines of customers. Being only a mile from downtown, Bouldin Creek has quickly become one of the most desirable residential neighborhoods in Austin. And although gentrification has pushed out some of the original eateries, it's still a great place to spend a day if your goal is to visit some classic Austin institutions. Many Bouldin Creek restaurants can be found on South 1st Street, which is considered the younger, quieter sister to the iconic South Congress Avenue just a few blocks away. Never fear: Although smaller and less crowded, South First boasts an equal number of impressive restaurants, bars, bakeries, food trucks, and breweries. Plan on a full day of eating, starting with breakfast, lunch, dessert, moving to happy hour and dinner, and maybe saving a little space for a late-night scoop of gelato.

1

START YOUR MORNING WITH A HOMEMADE VEGETARIAN BREAKFAST AT BOULDIN CREEK CAFE

Vegetarians and meat-eaters alike sprawl out in the hot Texas sun, waiting in the hours-long queue for a table at BOULDIN CREEK CAFE'S weekend breakfast. And although Sunday is the busiest meal of the week, that chipotle-pecan pesto can even make a Monday morning just a little bit brighter. This place is buzzing with south Austin vibes, starting with the "Caffeine Dealer" sign flashing toward South First Street.

Picture the likes of a young, tattooed singer/songwriter, donning an oversized hat and vintage sunglasses, recovering from performing a late Saturday night show on 6th Street and eager for her potato-pecan tamales with tofu scramble and an Earl Grey almond milk latte. This old-school Austin cafe serves omelets, sandwiches, breakfast tacos, and pastries for anyone who just wants good, homemade food. Yes, you can order dairy and eggs here, but even if you're not following a vegan lifestyle, try the tofu scramble at least once. You won't be sorry. And if you're overwhelmed by all the options in the pastry case, start with that giant, soft oatmeal cream sandwich cookie for a tasty vegan treat.

The drink menu offers locally roasted fair-trade coffee and over 20 varieties of tea, and the words "Hangover Helper!" in bright red illuminate the drink options for those who had just a little too much fun last night and need things like coconut water and Emergen-C. The indoor bar area is crowded from morning to night. Early risers get a caffeine fix to start the day, and the "funemployed" and free-lancers stop by during afternoon happy hour for cheap beer and wine.

Although Bouldin Creek Cafe is a wonderful breakfast spot for those who want to experience true south Austin, it is in no way a tour-ist trap. The same local customers come back week after week, year after year, eager to catch up with friends and indulge in homemade, hearty, healthy food.

Next up: another south Austin hot spot that has a crowd of happy customers at all hours of the day.

2 GRAB A PINT AT AMERICA'S FAVORITE BREWPUB, THE AUSTIN BEER GARDEN BREWING COMPANY

BBQ, breakfast tacos, craft beer: These are a few of the things that Austin can boast about, loud and proud. It's easy to find the best BBQ (Franklin), and breakfast tacos are simple enough (are the tortillas homemade? That's a good start.), but unless you're a serious craft beer drinker, you might have trouble choosing a brewery to visit among the seemingly endless number popping up in the greater Austin area.

Use their awards at the Great American Beer Fest (GABF) as a guide. The GABF is basically the Oscars for the craft beer world, and AUSTIN BEER GARDEN BREWING COMPANY has been winning gold medals for their beers for years. ABGBC specializes in German lagers, which are delicate, crisp beers that taste great by the pint or by the pitcher. Start with a pilsner or helles, which are both always on tap, then move on to try the rotating special beers.

In addition to award-winning beer (ABGBC has won "Large Brewpub of the Year" three years in a row), they also serve exceptional food. Big, chewy-crust pizzas are the main food of choice here. A handful of toppings are always available (Margherita, Calabrese, house-made sausage, among others), but the small number of special pies are where ABGB uses fresh,

seasonal ingredients to create layers of flavor that will surprise even the most seasoned pizza-eater.

Live music is played on the indoor stage every weekend; if you prefer a quieter dining experience, head outside to rows of picnic tables under twinkly lights. Both choices make for a perfect Austin evening.

Keep the food crawl moving for another beautiful Austin garden!

3

COZY UP NEXT TO YOUR DATE AT LENOIR

New American fare in a rustic chic setting makes **LENOIR** one of the most desirable and intimate dinner reservations in Austin. The restaurant can be broken into two parts: the small indoor dining room, which seats 32, and the larger backyard wine garden, which requires no reservations.

Lenoir's exterior is immediately recognizable: small, jagged pieces of whitewashed lumber are haphazardly nailed to create a wall that feels modern and simple. Step inside, and you are immediately greeted by . . . the entire restaurant. It is snug and relaxed. I have a theory that it is quite impossible to feel any stress at all while on Lenoir's property.

The husband/wife team behind this fantastic establishment is committed to sourcing from local farmers. Chef Todd Duplechan's "hot weather food" is meant to be grown, raised, and consumed in Texas. Guests can enjoy entrees a la carte, or a prix-fixe menu with wine pairings.

The outdoor wine garden is larger than the indoor dining area, though equally rustic and endearing. Lanterns and lights hang from decades-old live oak trees, illuminating white wooden tables and benches on a gravel floor. A small bar in the corner of the yard offers a lovely and exciting selection of wine, beer, and cider, as well as a few rotating snacks.

I'm an introvert, so I thrive on small gatherings with just one or two people from my tribe of friends. One of my happiest places is sitting in Lenoir's wine garden, sharing a bottle of bubbles and farmer veggies and *labneh* with friends on a hot summer night.

4

INDULGE IN AWARD-WINNING CUPCAKES AT SUGAR MAMA'S BAKESHOP

The cupcake craze took the United States by storm in the early 2000s. And while some massive cupcake chains did not manage to survive, Sugar Mama's is still thriving and selling out of popular cupcake flavors daily.

SUGAR MAMA'S is a small bakery in south Austin that makes absolutely everything from scratch. Waltz into the cute, colorful space and enjoy a James Brown (Valrhona chocolate cake topped with chocolate buttercream and sprinkles) or a classic Marilyn Monroe (buttery vanilla cupcakes with Madagascar bourbon vanilla buttercream) with a hot cup of coffee. If you find yourself in the shop on a day when they're offering the honey baklava, be sure to snag one; that's one of the cupcakes that helped Chef

Olivia O'Neal win first place on TV's *Cupcake Wars* in 2013.

Sugar Mama's does cupcakes really well, but it's a full-blown bakery, too. Pies, cookies, cakes, and bars also take up a hefty amount of space in the pastry case. The custom cake orders are perfect for birthdays and other special occasions.

The only complaint I have about Sugar Mama's is that I get too full before I get to taste all the cupcakes! My solution? Order a bunch, cut them into small pieces, and share with a group of friends.

"We opened Sugar Mama's Bakeshop in 2008 when Austin was on the verge of becoming the food-centric town it has evolved into. We opened with front-of-house experience, but very little back-of-house experience, and we had to learn as we went along!

"It has been both exciting and challenging to be a part of the food revolution here in the Bouldin Creek neighborhood. From the beginning we have had a focus on utilizing local (when possible), fair trade, and gourmet ingredients in all of our desserts. We are proud that we have never had to compromise in this area due to the ongoing support of the community in patronizing our business."

—*Olivia O'Neal,*
chef and owner of
Sugar Mama's Bakeshop

5

CELEBRATE SOMEONE SPECIAL AT MATTIE'S AT GREEN PASTURES

Most people don't expect to see peacocks in a central Texas city, but step onto MATTIE'S lawn and you'll witness a muster of long-tailed white and bright-blue birds strutting on the grassy carpet, proudly displaying their feathers. The peacocks are only one of the reasons why wandering onto Mattie's property feels a bit like walking into another world.

Unlike most Bouldin Creek restaurants, which are located on South 1st Street, Mattie's is nestled between houses in a residential neighborhood. The mansion, built around 1895, was originally home to Martha "Mattie" Faulk, and her husband, Henry. Though the original restaurant, Green Pastures, has recently been updated and renamed, the bones of the house remain. As does the famous 1965 Milk Punch on the cocktail menu. It's a creamy, booze-filled treat with sweet cream, bourbon and rum, maple, and a sprinkle of fresh nutmeg on top.

The multilevel interior has grand windows, creaking wooden floors, and lots of rooms for dining space. The lawn, which has its own happy hour menu, is a darling place to gather with family, open a bottle of wine, and make a toast to life.

Mattie's menu pays homage to its former life as Green Pastures by offering spruced-up versions of classic Southern dishes. Try the pimento

cheese, the buttermilk biscuits with local honey, or the famous Mattie's Fried Chicken.

Enjoy dessert here, or venture on to the next stop to taste some authentic Italian gelato.

Mattie's Famous 1965 Milk Punch

Mattie's Beverage Director Jason Stevens resurrected the original 1965 milk punch recipe, using only highest quality booze, rich, fresh milk, and freshly grated nutmeg.

Ingredients:
4 ounces Buffalo Trace bourbon
3 ounces Pierre Ferrand 1840 cognac
1½ ounces Appleton Reserve Jamaican rum
16 ounces half and half
8 ounces whole milk
2½ ounces grade A or B maple syrup
2 ounces Tempus Fugit crème de cacao
1 ounce quality vanilla paste
Whole nutmeg, for grating

Directions:
Combine all ingredients except for the nutmeg in a pitcher and stir vigorously to make sure the vanilla is fully dispersed in the mix.

Serve very cold. Dispense 1965 Milk Punch into small, chilled cups and then grate fresh nutmeg over each serving.

Recipe makes enough to serve a group of 4–6.

6

END YOUR NIGHT WITH A SCOOP OF AUTHENTIC ITALIAN GELATO AT DOLCE NEVE GELATO

In a city that experiences summer weather for about 75 percent of the year, a good gelato shop is a must. Thankfully, a sweet trio of Italians decided to open a shop in Bouldin Creek that offers the best gelato you'll find in town.

DOLCE NEVE
local·italian·gelato

The phrase "We do it in front of everyone" is displayed at the entrance for all to see. Directly underneath the sign, store employees are often churning fresh batches of gelato, sorbet, waffle cones, and other frozen snacks to serve each day.

Don't be surprised by the teeny sizes offered; gelato is dense, tightly packed into the small cups, and a little goes a long way. A combination of staples, rotating flavors, and seasonal flavors entices curious customers who stumble into the tiny, bright building. My personal favorite flavors? Anything with cheese: fromage blanc, goat cheese, ricotta, or mascarpone!

We do it in front of everyone

Authentic Italian gelato should meet a few criteria, and Dolce Neve checks everything off this list:

Natural flavors and colors. If you see oddly bright colors that wouldn't naturally occur from the ingredients (like bright green mint or hot pink strawberry gelato), they probably used artificial coloring.

Gelato that's stored in metal tins with lids, which help regular the temperature of the delicate dessert. Gelato, which is made with a lower fat content than ice cream, has to be served slightly warmer. To ensure the optimal temperatures, a great gelato shop like Dolce Neve stores the cold treat at a careful temperature. (Beware of those big fluffy mounds showcased behind glass; they're probably full of artificial fillers.)

Traditional flavors (think: stracciatella, pistachio, chocolate), as well as a few unique ones.

THE SOUTH LAMAR CRAWL

1. Cozy up with a coffee and a homemade biscuit and jam at **CONFITURAS LITTLE KITCHEN**, 2129 GOODRICH AVE., AUSTIN, (512) 710-9370, CONFITURAS.NET

2. Kick off the weekend with a farm-to-table brunch at **ODD DUCK**, 1201 S. LAMAR BLVD., AUSTIN, (512) 433-6512, ODDDUCKAUSTIN.COM

3. Lunch at **CHI'LANTRO BBQ**, HOME OF THE ORIGINAL KIMCHI FRIES, 1509 S. LAMAR BLVD., AUSTIN, (512) 428-5269, CHILANTROBBQ.COM

4. Take your pick of booze or caffeine at **RADIO COFFEE AND BEER**, 4204 MANCHACA RD., AUSTIN, (512) 394-7844, RADIOCOFFEEANDBEER.COM

5. Indulge in a memorable sushi dinner at **UCHI**, 801 S. LAMAR BLVD., AUSTIN, (512) 916-4808, UCHIAUSTIN.COM

6. Slurp a bowl of late-night noodles at **RAMEN TATSU-YA**, 1234 S. LAMAR BLVD., AUSTIN, (512) 893-5561, RAMEN-TATSUYA.COM

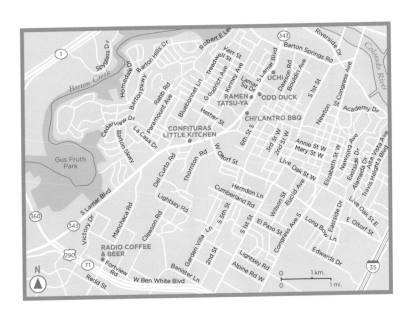

South Lamar

Party with the Young Professionals

SOUTH LAMAR (OR SOLA) IS BORDERED BY ZILKER ON THE WEST and Bouldin Creek on the east, which are both full of pricey urban single-family homes. But South Lamar, with its trendy apartment buildings and buzzing bar and restaurant scene, attracts 20- and 30-somethings who are often moving to Austin for the first time and want to live close to downtown in a more budget-friendly zone.

Old Austin charm still shines through amid the glitzy, high-rise apartments and mixed-use developments.

Here's an example: Far down south at the end of SoLa, just before the street runs into Ben White Boulevard, you'll find a small country dance hall called The Broken Spoke. It's squeezed between two towering mixed-use developments that offer living, retail, and work space. Although the space around The Broken Spoke is constantly evolving, the building and the clientele have hardly changed since it opened in 1964; it's still Austin's favorite place to dress in Western wear, two-step, and drink Shiner Bock. What has changed, though, is that you can now leave the dance hall and find world-renowned restaurants, coffee shops, food trucks, and bars on South Lamar Boulevard.

1

COZY UP WITH COFFEE AND A HOMEMADE BISCUIT AND JAM AT CONFITURAS LITTLE KITCHEN

CONFITURAS is Austin's first jam and biscuit shop, and it is absolutely charming! Owner Stephanie McClenney started Confituras from her kitchen in 2010 as a way to preserve all the delicious produce that she found at the Austin farmers markets. Her company grew, and grew, and grew, picking up awards along the way, and she was finally able to open a brick-and-mortar just off South Lamar.

Although the company started by making jams, jellies, and preserves, and selling them in the farmers' markets and grocery stores around Austin (including Whole Foods and Antonelli's Cheese Shop), the team at Confituras decided they wanted to offer more than just jam in the new store.

Jam needs a vehicle to get from jar to mouth, and biscuits were the perfect solution. Confituras sells flaky, buttery biscuits that can be enjoyed in the store or ordered by the dozen to take away. Be sure to browse around and find a jar of jam to take home with you, too!

Confituras is special because they use local ingredients and their jams follow the seasons, which means the flavors and colors are exceptional. The options are anything but boring: Try Bourbon Brown Sugar Peach Preserves in the summer, Grapefruit Vanilla Bean Jam in the winter, or (my very favorite) Salted Caramel Pear Butter on the first brisk autumn morning.

These sweet treats prime the appetite for the seasonal feast to come at the next stop on South Lamar.

2 KICK OFF THE WEEKEND WITH A FARM-TO-TABLE BRUNCH AT ODD DUCK

Bryce Gilmore, owner of ODD DUCK, is one of the pioneers of the farm-to-table movement in Austin. His mission to source seasonally from local farmers led to his opening a food truck in 2009, which became the brick-and-mortar Odd Duck in 2013.

The rustic charm of the restaurant matches the farm-to-table concept: Burlap-wrapped chandeliers hang from the ceiling and food is served on mismatched vintage dishware.

Sunday brunch is an event, and pastries are the star of the show. If your server walks by with a platter of them and you can't choose just one, always go for more, not less. You can just bring them home to enjoy with coffee the next day.

Odd Duck recommends that you order a selection of small plates, making this a great place to dine with close friends and family. If you love sharing food, this place is for you.

The menu changes with the seasons, so you know you'll always get whatever is fresh. If you're stumped by the menu, ask your server for recommendations, or look at the photos on Odd Duck's Instagram account (@oddduckaustin) for stunning shots of the latest and greatest menu items.

The truck-to-table trend continues with the next stop, Chi'Lantro.

3

LUNCH AT CHI'LANTRO BBQ, HOME OF THE ORIGINAL KIMCHI FRIES

There's a trend in Austin of a food truck opening up, seizing the city's attention by cooking excellent, creative food, and then turning into a successful brick-and-mortar business with multiple locations. Example: CHI'LANTRO.

Korean BBQ meets Mexican food at this fusion-fare hot spot on SoLa. They're "Home of the Original Kimchi Fries," which are an absolute must-try menu item for the first-time customer. What exactly are kimchi fries, you ask? Chi'Lantro starts with a heap of thick fries, covers them with your choice of protein (spicy pork or chicken, soy-glazed chicken, tofu, or rib-eye beef), and tops the whole thing with caramelized kimchi, cheese, onions, cilantro, magic sauce, sesame seeds, and sriracha. It's a completely justifiable way to count fries as a complete meal.

Other favorites are the popular tacos, bowls, queso, and wings; they all take a basic concept and spin it through a mix of cultures to create a delectable, memorable, completely Insta-worthy meal. The Chi'Jeu Queso with the optional rib-eye beef (it's optional, but . . . it's really not!) is a must-order menu item.

Although this food truck has expanded into a business with several brick-and-mortars, the food truck is still available for catering at private events. My husband and I love the kimchi fries so much, we decided to hire the food truck to serve them for dinner at our 2017 wedding!

Let's keep this party going and roll on over to Radio Coffee and Beer.

4

TAKE YOUR PICK OF BOOZE OR CAFFEINE AT RADIO COFFEE AND BEER

Follow South Lamar until it splits into two roads, and follow the eastern road, Manchaca, until you eventually run into a hybrid coffee shop and beer garden. It's nestled under a shady grove of trees that provides a canopy over the sprawling outdoor patio, and it's consistently crowded with regulars.

Folks gather at RADIO COFFEE AND BEER morning, noon, and night for caffeine, beer, live music, food trucks, and a comfortable gathering place to meet up with friends. The renovated house provides a cool space for working quietly on a laptop, joining a group for trivia night, and listening to a bluegrass band play on the small corner stage.

Radio is an all-day coffee shop and bar, which means they have drinks for any hour of the day. A full coffee program using Stumptown beans will get you started with a caffeine kick in the morning. Meeting a buddy in the afternoon? Get some *kombucha* or nitro cold brew on tap. For folks who visit Radio at night, the beer selection provides a peek into the vast craft beer scene in Austin. Try pours from popular Austin breweries like St. Elmo, Blue Owl, and Hops and Grain.

Another huge draw of Radio, of course, is the selection of food trucks parked outside. Order a yummy breakfast sandwich at Paperboy or a few tacos at Veracruz

All Natural. The *migas* taco from Veracruz is a must-try menu item; it's widely recognized as Austin's favorite *migas* taco, which is quite a bold statement for this taco-saturated city to make. Pair it with a cappuccino for the ultimate start to your day.

5

INDULGE IN A MEMORABLE SUSHI DINNER AT UCHI

Ask any Austin foodie what her favorite sushi restaurant is, and UCHI is sure to be come up in the conversation. Uchi is not just the most popular sushi restaurant in Austin: It's one of the most popular restaurants, period. (Make dinner reservations weeks in advance!)

Chef Tyson Cole, who received the prestigious James Beard Foundation Award for Best Chef: Southwest, spent years of his life learning all about the Japanese sushi tradition under masters in Tokyo, New York, and Austin before founding Uchi in 2003.

The experienced sushi eater will enjoy ordering individual items for a meal. But if you're not familiar with sushi culture and just want to sit back and enjoy, the 10-course omakase chef's tasting menu is a great way to experience all that Uchi has to offer. Plate after plate will be placed in front of you, explained in detail, and left for you to devour.

One of the huge draws to Uchi, especially among the younger crowd, is their "Sake Social Hour" which takes place from 5 to 6:30 pm every day. It's their version of a happy hour, and it is, by far, the best way to experience Uchi on a budget. The menu consists of about 10 hot and cold menu items and a selection of discounted sake.

Enjoy Uchi with an open mind and eagerness to try something different. The food will surprise and delight you.

6

SLURP A BOWL OF LATE-NIGHT NOODLES AT RAMEN TATSU-YA

Austin has become the proud home to all sorts of types of ramen, with thin, thick, or curly noodles, from velvety rich tonkotsu pork bone broth to subtle shio chicken-based broth, *tsukemen* dipping noodles, and even vegetarian and vegan variations.

But if you just have time for one bowl of ramen, and you're not sure where to go, here's my best suggestion: Stop by RAMEN TATSU-YA on your journey down South Lamar.

What makes this place so special? Co-owners Tatsu Aikawa and Takuya "Tako" Matsumoto take pride in their specialty: *tonkotsu*. This is a creamy ramen from Kyushu, Japan, which simmers up to 60 hours in order to summon the flavors of each ingredient. Pork fat permeates every ounce of broth, making this giant bowl of broth and noodles one of the most delectable comfort foods you can find in Austin.

When you're ready to order, there are several options. *Tonkotsu* is Tatsu-ya's strong suit; Tatsu and Tako spent months perfecting the complexities of the broth, noodles, and toppings. From there, you might wish to venture to the Tonkotsu-Shoyu, which adds

> **Is your ramen vocabulary ready for Tatsu-ya?**
>
> *Tonkotsu:* A rich, slow-cooked broth made from simmering pork bones and fat. Not to be confused with tonkatsu, a popular fried pork cutlet dish.
>
> *Shio:* A clear, thin broth with salt added.
>
> *Miso:* A fermented soybean broth, typically paired with heavy meat like pork; can also be spicy.
>
> *Chashu:* Soy-braised pork belly.
>
> *Kikurage:* Wood-ear mushroom.

a decadent soy sauce blend to the pork bone broth, or try a Mi-So-Not (mild) or Mi-So-Hot (spicy) for a broth made with fermented soybean.

Broth and noodles are the stars of the show, but ramen is more exciting with some fun toppings; try ordering several to find your own personal favorites! Certain toppings come standard at Tastu-ya, like the *chashu* (soy braised pork belly) and *ajitama* (marinated soft-boiled egg), but I also like to add a spicy bomb of red pepper paste, corn with brown butter, and an extra sheet of nori.

THE DOWNTOWN AUSTIN CRAWL

1. Enjoy an expertly prepared pour-over coffee at **HOUNDSTOOTH COFFEE**, 401 CONGRESS AVE. #100C, AUSTIN, (512) 394-6051, HOUNDSTOOTHCOFFEE.COM

2. Stop by **WALTON'S FANCY AND STAPLE** for a lazy weekday breakfast, 609 W. 6TH ST., AUSTIN, (512) 542-3380, WALTONSFANCYANDSTAPLE.COM

3. Linger over margaritas and modern Mexican cuisine at the beautiful **LA CONDESA**, 400 W. 2ND ST., AUSTIN, (512) 499-0300, LACONDESA.COM

4. Sneak in a predinner martini at **SMALL VICTORY**, 108 E. 7TH ST., AUSTIN, SMALLVICTORY.BAR

5. Marvel at the modern Southern food creations at **OLAMAIE**, 1610 SAN ANTONIO ST., AUSTIN, (512) 474-2796, OLAMAIEAUSTIN.COM

6. Play some ping-pong with friends at creek-side beer garden **EASY TIGER**, 709 E. 6TH ST., AUSTIN, (512) 614-4972, EASYTIGERAUSTIN.COM

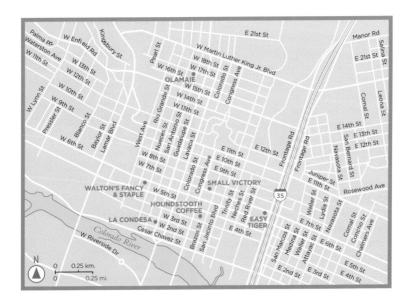

Downtown Austin

Where Austinites Live, Work, and Play

DOWNTOWN AUSTIN TRULY IS THE CENTER OF THE CITY. When Edwin Waller, the first Mayor of Austin, was asked to construct a new town in the 1830s, he chose the 15 square blocks between Shoal and Waller Creek (east to west) and 15th Street and the Colorado River (north to south) that now make up the majority of downtown.

While you can still find historical landmarks, office buildings, and shopping districts, it is massive residential towers that have been filling Austin in the past decade. As more people call downtown Austin home, the restaurant and bar scene has been consistently opening more options to accommodate the increasing foot traffic.

Downtown Austin can be broken into several districts for easy navigation:

SECOND STREET DISTRICT: Get your retail therapy on! This is downtown Austin's largest shopping street.

HISTORIC 6TH STREET DISTRICT: Austin's go-to party street for live music and bars. A few blocks are closed to vehicular traffic on weekend nights to make this a safe place for pedestrians to bar hop.

SEAHOLM DISTRICT: Formerly home of the Seaholm Power Plant, this area has been renovated and is now a beautiful place to live, shop, and eat.

RED RIVER DISTRICT: home to several of the city's hottest night clubs including Stubb's, Barbarella, and Mohawk.

CONGRESS AVENUE: originally the largest north-south street in Austin, running from Congress on the north and the Colorado River on the south. It's now a home to historical sites like the state capitol and the Paramount Theater. (Congress was later extended south of the river; go to page 51 to read about South Congress Avenue!)

And of course, there's Rainey Street, which we'll cover in another chapter. That street deserves its own day of eating!

1

ENJOY AN EXPERTLY PREPARED POUR-OVER COFFEE AT HOUNDSTOOTH COFFEE

Walk into **HOUNDSTOOTH,** and you're guaranteed an exceptional cup of coffee. But more than that, you're guaranteed an experience. At this point in your coffee journey, you recognize that drinking coffee is about more than just getting caffeinated in the morning. It's about connecting with humans, and Houndstooth has the friendliest baristas (and the best coffee program) in Austin.

Houndstooth was at the forefront of the specialty coffee movement in Austin. What started as a single cafe in north Austin has now expanded across Texas, including several cafes that serve cocktails. The Congress Avenue location is an energizing place to start your morning before exploring the rest of downtown Austin. It's tucked into the corner of a high-rise office building, and there's a steady stream of people making their way in and out the door. Bright music plays on a speaker, and the bold red wall at the front stands out amid the otherwise neutral, calming tones of the cafe.

As you make a selection for a pour-over or an espresso-based drink, a barista will gladly help you navigate through various roasts that are

offered on the menu. This is especially great if you're new to coffee and need help exploring the subtle variations in mouthfeel and flavor profiles. And maybe you're not interested in "fancy" coffee and you just want a quick cup to wake you up? There's always the batch brew, kept fresh throughout the morning and easy to order.

There are also some seasonal drink items that are fun to try. They change every few months, so no guarantees on what will be available when you stop by, but they're always clever concoctions that start with a coffee base. One of the most unusual drinks they offer is the limeade and black coffee blend!

If you want to take your coffee to go, Houndstooth is just three short blocks from the hike and bike trail at Lady Bird Lake. Enjoy a morning stroll before diving into an epic downtown Austin breakfast feast.

"The Pattern of Coffee and People." What does Houndstooth Coffee's motto mean, anyway?

"At Houndstooth we believe each interaction has the potential to be a memorable, venerable moment to be weaved in the Pattern of Coffee and People. We get 30 seconds to a minute each day with people, but over months and years, those moments develop into an intricate and beautiful pattern of taking care of our guests."

—Paul Henry, Houndstooth co-founder

2 STOP BY WALTON'S FANCY AND STAPLE FOR A LAZY WEEKDAY BREAKFAST

WALTON'S FANCY AND STAPLE is a restaurant, bakery, and gift shop in a historic Sixth Street building. It's the combination of two Austin institutions—Walton's Florist and Nursery, and Fischer Brothers Grocery, and it has a nostalgic general-store feel with an elegant twist. Make a quick stop for coffee and pastries in the morning, or enjoy a classy lunch of gourmet deli sandwiches and dainty French macarons. The large chalkboard menu features breakfast staples like challah French toast, cranberry-pecan praline oatmeal, and shrimp and smoked Gouda grits. The cold sandwiches, pressed panini, soups, and salads provide a vast assortment of tasty lunch options.

Right when you walk in, the glass cases near the entrance will tempt you with all sorts of colorful sweets and treats, like salty oat cookies, cream cheese brownies, and Walton's famous Honey-Bee Cake, a honey-almond cake layered with caramel buttercream and topped with ganache. Don't miss out on the Golden Eggs, which are nutmeg-infused yellow cakes dipped in melted butter and coated in cinnamon and sugar. Whether you're stopping for a full meal or just a little bite to take on the road, this is a great place to pick up a scrumptious treat, unique souvenir, or a bouquet of flowers for a friend.

3

LINGER OVER MARGARITAS AND INTERIOR MEXICAN CUISINE AT THE BEAUTIFUL LA CONDESA

The restaurant scene in downtown Austin is constantly turning over and creating new concepts, but the modern interior Mexican cuisine at LA CONDESA has remained a favorite among locals and visitors alike for the past decade. This bright, lively spot in the heart of downtown has the trifecta of a perfect dining experience: quality food, exceptional hospitality, and a beautiful ambience.

If you've never experienced a flight of mezcal, this is the place to try it: La Condesa features the largest selection of 100 percent blue agave tequila and mezcal in Austin. Not interested in drinking it straight? The cocktail list full of fun drinks, like El Cubico, made with tobacco-infused Cazadores Reposado and vanilla-infused brandy.

This is one of the few restaurants in Austin where I enjoy the bar experience just as much as the actual restaurant. The starters are creative and satisfying as appetizers for a meal, or perfect as a small meal enjoyed at the counter. Try all four creative flavors of guacamole in the guacamole tasting, the bright tiradito ceviche with *hamachi*, ginger, and charred scallion vinaigrette, or the Zanahoria Salad with roasted Texas carrots and crispy quinoa.

The homemade corn tortillas are perfect for scooping up every last little bit of the slowly cooked mole or the crowd-favorite lamb *barbacoa*. And for those who need a smaller plate, the tacos and tostadas are made with delightful, locally sourced ingredients.

Boca Negra is La Condesa's flourless chocolate cake, and it makes the perfect, spicy ending to the meal. Chef Rick Lopez kicks it up a notch by adding chile de arbor, ancho, and covering it with caramelized banana and brown sugar–banana ice cream.

No need to end the good times yet! Enjoy a short 10-minute walk to get to some of Austin's best martinis.

4

SNEAK IN A PRE-DINNER MARTINI AT SMALL VICTORY

The first time I went to SMALL VICTORY, I walked right past it before realizing I had arrived. The sign on the door is small, and the windowless second-story bar is invisible from the street, but these expertly prepared cocktails have become an Austin favorite for pre- or post-dinner drinks.

Owners Josh Loving and Brian Stubbs have worked in some of the most impressive cocktail bars in Austin, like Weather Up and Midnight Cowboy, and they know that a dark and sultry speakeasy atmosphere is cool, but the backbone of a great cocktail bar has to come from great drinks. Their progressive ice program means that all of the ice is made in-house. The result? Your drink will be prepared as cold as possible, without being

watered down by ice that melts too quickly.

Each menu item has a color illustration, a list of ingredients, and a short description of origin. Although I'm not typically one to go for tiki drinks, Small Victory's Hurricane, originating from Pat O'Brien's in New Orleans, is made with Jamaican rum and house-made passion fruit syrup. It's classy, a little sassy, and won't make you feel like the odd one out if you want a sweet drink while everyone else is sipping gin martinis.

Speaking of martinis, Small Victory is undoubtedly the best place to order one in Austin. The martini menu is illustrated as a flowchart to walk you through your choices (Gin or vodka; degree of dryness; twist, olive, or onion?) so you can place an order in full confidence.

If you need some nourishment to go with your booze, small plates of Antonelli's cheese, charcuterie, olives, and nuts are available. Save some room for dinner, though; there are plenty of award-winning dinner restaurants in downtown Austin, and Olamaie is at the top of the list.

5

MARVEL AT THE MODERN SOUTHERN FOOD CREATIONS AT OLAMAIE

OLAMAIE is an upscale Southern restaurant from James Beard Award–nominated chef Michael Fojtasek, and the first thing you need to know about this place is that you cannot leave without tasting the off-the-menu biscuits.

No matter if you've made reservations for Sunday brunch, a formal weekend date night, or just a regular Tuesday night dinner, the biscuits must be ordered. They're soft, buttery pillows of dough that hardly need any toppings, but the honey butter served on the side doesn't hurt.

Although the concept is elevated Southern cuisine, don't expect to recognize the menu items as stereotypical Southern food.

The unassuming white bungalow that houses Olamaie has housed many different concepts in its years, but step inside the newly designed space and you'll experience an air of celebration. This is no dingy, dusty, Southern restaurant; Olamaie's interior bright white walls, taupe accents, and tufted bench seats feel give off a feeling of sophistication. Enter the restaurant by walking through a winding porch and a charming sitting area. Waiting for a table? Treat yourself to one of their beautiful cocktails or a homemade soda to pass the time.

The food menu shifts with the seasons, and the ingredients are local, sourced within 200 miles of Austin. This restaurant is about the entire experience, so plan on enjoying predinner drinks, appetizers (hint: BISCUITS!), several dishes to share, and a lovely Southern dessert of zucchini bread with honeycomb ice cream.

Downtown Austin is full of all sorts of late-night hangout spots, and the one with the most chill is, ironically, at the very end of the craziest party street in Austin.

6 PLAY SOME PING-PONG WITH FRIENDS AT CREEK-SIDE BEER GARDEN EASY TIGER

Walk into the ground-floor level of **EASY TIGER** Bakeshop, and you'll instantly be hit with a wall of aroma that is so strong, toasty, and comforting that any thought you might have had about resisting carbs that day . . . *poof*. Gone, like a cloud of flour in the air.

The three-level shop that makes up Easy Tiger consists of a bakeshop, a bakery, a bar, a creek-side beer garden, and a restaurant. Easy Tiger is small but mighty: The kitchen makes more than 13,000 breads and rolls per week and another 4,500 pastries, and their bread is shipped all over Austin to be sold in more than 40 grocery stores and restaurants. Although additional Easy Tiger locations have now opened, the original 6th Street store is the one that stole the hearts of Austinites when it opened in 2012.

If you're here for late-night bites, the snack board is a fun way to taste a little bit of everything: The chewy pretzels, Chex mix, beef jerky, beer cheese, and Brooklyn lager mustard are fun to pair with one of the many draught beer options. All of Easy Tiger's sausages can be served on pretzel buns. I love dunking mine in any extra beer cheese! And the sandwiches, which are all made with in-house prepared meat, are piled high with tasty ingredients like sauerkraut, corned beef, pastrami, sour cream horseradish, and spicy pickled vegetables, all served on toasty Easy Tiger bread.

The creek-side patio is a safe haven amidst the craziness of "Dirty Sixth" Street. While the loud bars with their stumbling partygoers and pulsing bass beats are just a few blocks down the road, Easy Tiger nurtures a more relaxed, friendly vibe with ping-pong tables, hanging lights, and rows of creek-side picnic tables that are ready to welcome you and your friends with a cold pint of beer.

THE RAINEY STREET CRAWL

1. Take on the largest tap wall in Austin at BANGERS SAUSAGE HOUSE AND BEER GARDEN, 79 RAINEY ST., AUSTIN, (512) 432-5533, BANGERSAUSTIN.COM

2. Enjoy the laid-back hospitality at G'RAJ MAHAL, 73 RAINEY ST., AUSTIN, (512) 480-2255, GARAJMAHALAUSTON.COM

3. Sip on Rainey's best cocktails at HALF STEP, 75½ RAINEY ST., AUSTIN, (512) 391-1877, HALFSTEPBAR.COM

4. Taste bites of farm-to-table fare served from a dim sum cart at EMMER & RYE, 51 RAINEY ST. #110, AUSTIN, (512) 366-5530, EMMERANDRYE .COM

5. Still hungry? Nosh on thick-crust pizza with your beer at CRAFT PRIDE, 61 RAINEY ST., AUSTIN, (512) 428-5571, CRAFTPRIDEAUSTIN.COM

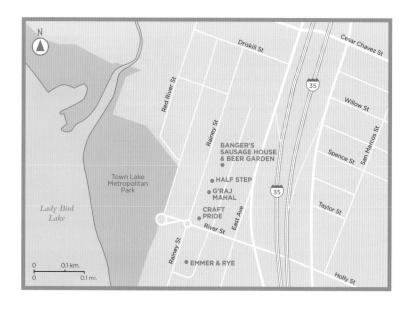

Rainey Street

Bars and Bungalows

ALTHOUGH IT IS TECHNICALLY A PART OF DOWNTOWN AUSTIN, Rainey Street has earned its own chapter in this book because it's the most concentrated area of bars, restaurants, and food trucks in the city.

What used to be a sleepy residential street has gradually been transformed into Austin's hottest nightlife scene. The small, one-story bungalows that quietly lined Rainey Street were excellent candidates to be renovated into quirky bars. Each one has its own theme, and many of them have darling front patios and huge backyard spaces for yard games or intimate concerts.

Of course, as the street has gradually shifted from residential to commercial, the need for high-rise living and hotels has skyrocketed. Several new builds provide living space above and retail for restaurants below. This adds a modern element to the street. Walk up and down Rainey, and you'll see that it's a beautiful jumble of design ideas.

Those who aren't quite rowdy (or brave!) enough to take on the "Dirty Sixth" Street bar scene will find a bit of peace on Rainey Street. You'll find everyone from bachelor and bachelorette parties, college students, mature couples, visitors in town for SXSW, and locals who know the area and love visiting their favorite bar on any night of the week.

1

TAKE ON THE LARGEST TAP WALL IN AUSTIN AT BANGER'S SAUSAGE HOUSE AND BEER GARDEN

Bar-hopping on Rainey Street with a crowd? BANGER'S is your place. All of the seating is made up of long rows of picnic tables, making this an easy bet for your hungry party of 10.

As the name suggests, the restaurant mostly serves sausage and beer. All 30 varieties of sausage are made in-house, and the tap list is in the triple digits. When I'm eager to drink beer from around the globe, I'll head to Banger's. This is the largest tap wall in the entire city of Austin! You'll be able to taste local craft beer from Austin as well as brews from around the world.

The sausage menu starts with the most basic offerings for those who want something familiar: bratwurst, andouille sausage, and smoked hot dogs made from beef and veal. The Italian sausage and peppers is flavorful meal with its hefty serving of bell peppers and onions cooked al dente, topped with aromatic cracked black pepper and torn basil.

Keep reading down the menu, and the sausage names get more and more eclectic. (Just one more restaurant doing its part to "Keep Austin Weird," folks!) Try the duck, bacon, and fig sausage for a sweet/savory combo, or the rabbit and mushroom, which is ground with shiitake mushrooms, Manchego cheese, and plenty of garlic. The other can't-miss menu

items are fried cheese curds, a big hearty plate of *poutine*, and the jalapeño mac and cheese.

Like most Rainey Street bars, this one has a stage nestled into the corner of the backyard. Live music fills the air, and beer and good times are flowing. I'll cheers to that.

The next Rainey stop is just a few steps away, but a world away in regard to cuisine!

2

ENJOY THE LAID-BACK HOSPITALITY
AT G'RAJ MAHAL

Even from its early days as a food truck, G'RAJ MAHAL has always been a charmer. Kind hospitality, warm, soothing food that's cooked to order, and an offbeat yet memorable name make this Austin-Indian restaurant a delightful lunch stop during your Rainey Street food crawl. Chef Sidney Roberts cooks food from the western region of India, (with a few uniquely "Austin" twists) with beef and pork that are locally sourced and chicken and goat that are grass-fed and halal-blessed. The samosas are stuffed with your choice of filling (goat, lamb, spinach and paneer, or potato and pea), fried to a deep, crunchy brown, and served with a variety of yummy chutneys. One bite of those samosas and you'll understand why they're the most popular

starters here. The menu has an impressive number of noncream and cream curries, all with varying spice level. (Just tell your server how much spice you can handle, and the kitchen will take it from there.) I love keeping things simple and ordering the tikka masala, a creamy tomato base with onions, peppers, and a choice of protein. It's so delicious with a big piece of fresh naan to scoop up every last little bit of sauce. If you want to try something a bit wilder, though, there are 12 curries in all to help you taste every flavor of western Indian cuisine.

The front porch overlooks busy Rainey Street, and the back patio is an adorable place to dine with a big group of friends. Inside the cute bungalow-turned-restaurant is more seating and a corner bar with wine and beer offerings. The ambience at G'Raj Mahal lends itself to an excellent afternoon of sharing food.

No need to save any room for food: The next stop on Rainey Street is for cocktails.

3

SIP ON RAINEY'S BEST COCKTAILS AT HALF STEP

You can order a decent drink at almost any bar on Rainey, but if you're looking for an exceptional craft cocktail, one bar stands far above the rest: **HALF STEP**. *Esquire* magazine called this one of the best bars in the country.

What makes these cocktails so exceptional? Half Step gives special attention to an often-overlooked component of the cocktail: ice. Half Step is one of the few bars in Texas that makes its ice completely in-house, from start to finish. They start with an extensive filtration process, then freeze the water into massive, 350-pound blocks of clear ice. Using a mod-ified band saw, they cut the ice into five custom shapes to be used for various cocktails. When you walk into the bar, you're ordering a cocktail that is not only made with homemade juices and syrups, but also home-grown ice.

With an ice program this elab-orate, you might expect an air of

YOU'RE VISITING A US HISTORIC DISTRICT!

The Rainey Street Historic District includes 120 acres.

The street was added to the National Register of Historic Places in 1985.

There are 31 buildings on Rainey that were built before 1934.

Most of the homes on Rainey Street are bungalow-style, which is just the right size to be renovated into stylish bars!

pretention among the bartenders. But you'll only find warm hospitality at Half Step. This is a neighborhood bar. Whether you order a vodka soda or a Reposado Martinez with tequila *reposado*, Punt e Mes, maraschino, and mole bitters, your drink will be prepared with the utmost care.

The draft cocktails are an easy place to start. The Ginger Paloma, made with tequila, ginger, lime, grapefruit, and Mexican grapefruit soda, is refreshing on a warm Austin evening. If you choose to stray from the menu, have a chat with your bartender. Discuss your favorite cocktail ingredients, pick a spirit, and ask him to create a cocktail based on those.

Now that you've imbibed award-winning cocktails, it's time to dine at an award-winning restaurant.

4 TASTE BITES OF FARM-TO-TABLE FARE SERVED FROM A DIM SUM CART AT EMMER & RYE

As the name suggests, the focus at EMMER & RYE is on the house-milled heirloom grains. This means that not only is the pasta home-made, but the flour to make the pasta is also milled right there in the restaurant.

The menu rotates with the seasons, but one menu item never gets cut: the Blue Beard Durum *cacio e pepe*. *Cacio e pepe* is a simple dish of pasta, cheese, and black pepper, but Emmer & Rye puts so much detail into preparing their chewy pasta and rich, creamy cheese, just order it and you'll see why this dish is a customer favorite. After my first bite, I made it a goal to order *cacio e pepe* around the country, trying to find one that matches the same quality of texture and flavor that Emmer & Rye can produce in their dish; I've had no luck thus far.

Perhaps one of the most unusual aspects of Emmer & Rye is the rolling dim sum cart, which will be wheeled up to your table several times throughout dinner service. Chef Kevin Fink, who was nominated for a James Beard Award, recognized that there are a lot of unknowns in the food industry; a fisherman could score a great catch that morning, or a farm could yield a particularly excellent crop, best used that same day. He wanted to be able to feature different menu items based on what was freshest on that

particular day. These off-menu items, which are carefully explained by a knowledgeable server, often end up being my favorite bites of the meal.

The night doesn't have to end here! Walk across the street to experience the most distinctively Texas craft beer bar in Austin.

5

STILL HUNGRY? NOSH ON THICK–CRUST PIZZA WITH YOUR BEER AT CRAFT PRIDE

Brewery-hopping in Austin is fun, but what if you could taste a whole slew of Texas craft beers at one bar? That's where CRAFT PRIDE comes in to play.

Fifty-four taps of craft beer, all brewed in Texas, line the front wall of the dark, cozy bar. The flights are a great way to compare and contrast a variety of Texas beer. The large menu over the tap wall is organized by flavor profile (light, malty, hoppy, wheats, sours, etc.) so you can find the drink that speaks to your soul.

Step out the back door and you'll find a giant patio and backyard surrounded by a tall wooden fence. There's a permanent food trailer by the name of Via 313 parked in the corner that serves genuine Detroit-style pizza. This square pizza is made on a thick and chewy Sicilian crust, a thick layer of pepperoni, and lots of hot, bubbling cheese. Of course, there are plenty of options if pepperoni isn't your thing. The Cadillac is a unique sweet take on pizza, made with Gorgonzola, fig preserves, prosciutto di Parma, Parmesan, and balsamic glaze. If you're drinking hoppy

beer and want a more classic pizza experience, give the Detroiter a try. It's a pepperoni lover's dream with smoked pepperoni under the cheese and natural-casing pepperoni on top.

If you're lucky, a band will be performing live music while you enjoy your hot pizza and cold brews. Texas craft beer, live music, and a patio covered in twinkly lights? Welcome to the ultimate Saturday night in Austin.

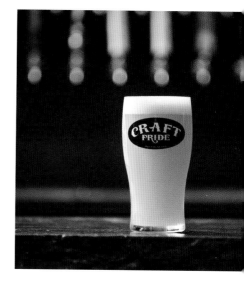

THE SOUTH CONGRESS CRAWL

1. Brunch in style at **CAFE NO SÉ**, 1603 S. CONGRESS AVE., AUSTIN, (512) 942-2061, CAFENOSEAUSTIN.COM

2. Chow down on an authentic New York–style pie at **HOME SLICE PIZZA**, 1415 S. CONGRESS AVE., AUSTIN, (512)-444-7437, HOMESLICEPIZZA.COM

3. Experience the famous flagship location of **TORCHY'S TACOS**, 1822 S. CONGRESS AVE., AUSTIN, (512) 916-9025, TORCHYSTACOS.COM

4. Grab your girlfriend and indulge in fries and rosé at **JUNE'S ALL DAY**, 1722 S. CONGRESS AVE., AUSTIN, (512) 416-1722, JUNESALLDAY.COM

5. Snack on Tokyo-inspired street food at **LUCKY ROBOT**, 1303 S. CONGRESS AVE., (512) 444-8081, LUCKYROBOTRESTAURANT.COM

6. Make your inner-child happy with a double (or triple) scoop at **AMY'S ICE CREAMS**, 1301 S. CONGRESS AVE., (512) 440-7488, AMYSICECREAMS.COM

7. Dress up for date night at **PERLA'S,** the finest seafood restaurant in Austin, 1400 S. CONGRESS AVE., AUSTIN, (512) 291-7300, PERLASAUSTIN.COM

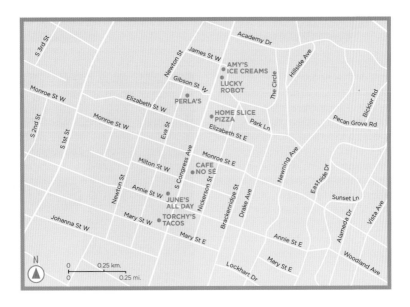

South Congress

Not Such a Tourist Trap

SOUTH CONGRESS AVENUE IS AUSTIN'S BIGGEST SHOPPING, entertainment, and tourist street, and it has a rich history. It was first paved with concrete in 1910 when a new bridge was built and streetcar lines were extended across the river, and since then it has continued to grow and evolve into what it is today. The South Congress Bridge, which stretches across Lady Bird Lake, is sometimes called the "bat bridge" because it's home to the largest urban bat colony in the world. If you're walking on a South Congress crosswalk and gaze north, you'll get a perfect view of the Texas State Capitol, which is the largest state capitol building in the country (just smaller than the US Capitol in Washington, DC).

SoCo is a good central "home base" for Austin visitors, with easy access to other parts of town and enough great restaurants to fill up a solid weekend of eating. I never get tired of wandering up and down the streets of SoCo on a busy Saturday morning, shopping and eating to my heart's content. Even though it's a trendy tourist area, South Congress has some of Austin's best restaurants where locals love hanging out. It's a brunch lover's paradise with multiple options (I'll mention two of them in this chapter), lots of happy hour hot spots, and some fine-dining establishments that are perfect for wrapping up your day of shopping.

1

BRUNCH IN STYLE AT CAFE NO SÉ

Cameras ready!

CAFE NO SÉ is a bright corner spot nestled into the bottom floor of the South Congress Hotel, where you're likely to find well-dressed individuals in vintage hats and trendy clothes gathering for a healthy or indulgent breakfast before starting their days. Nearly everything here (even the floor) is Instagrammable, making this the perfect place for those of us who love taking pictures of our food. A communal table in the middle of the room can seat a large group, and smaller tables are scattered around the indoor space and outdoor patio for quiet brunch-goers who are looking for a fresh, seasonal menu on SoCo.

The pastries from James Beard Foundation Award semifinalist Amanda Rockman are worth the indulgence; I love sharing them with the table so I'm still hungry for a brunch entree. The *kouign amann* is a must-try item: It's a flaky pastry with layers of butter and sugar and a chewy, caramelized exterior.

Healthy brunch options include avocado toast, which looks stunning with crème fraîche, arugula, and Aleppo carrots heaped on top, or a red quinoa porridge bowl with kiwi and toasted pistachio. If you're on vacation and simply want to indulge, the ricotta hotcakes are tall, fluffy pieces of heaven smothered in bananas, pecan butter, and maple syrup.

Not all of us are early morning risers, but thankfully Cafe No Sé offers an all-day menu that extends until 10 pm. Fuel up for a fun day of exploring SoCo!

2 CHOW DOWN ON AUTHENTIC NEW YORK–STYLE PIE AT HOME SLICE PIZZA

These homemade, thin-crust, hand-tossed pies have won the hearts of locals and visitors alike, as is apparent by the crowd lined up on the sidewalk, waiting for a table inside **HOME SLICE PIZZA**.

Home Slice became a south Austin favorite immediately after it opened in the early 2000s because of its catchy name, friendly service, and (of course), delicious pies. The pizza became so popular, in fact, that the team at Home Slice bought the space next door and opened "More Home Slice," a walk-up counter that offers pizza by the slice until the wee hours of the morning.

The menu, as with any traditional pizzeria, is fairly easy to navigate: The garlic knots with marinara and a big family-style salad are a great start to the meal. The thin, chewy-crust pizzas can be personalized with your own favorite toppings or enjoyed from the "tried and true" menu that Home Slice provides; these are classics like pepperoni and mushroom, white clam pizza, and eggplant pie. The sub sandwiches are the most overlooked menu items. The hot meatball sub is a soft and warm home-baked Italian roll filled with rich marinara sauce and oozy provolone, mozzarella, and Parmesan cheese and homemade meatballs. And I am slightly ashamed to admit that I was a regular customer here for five years before ever ordering the Italian sub. One bite of that fresh and chewy homemade bread full of a generous pile of Italian meat and cheese, and the cravings haven't stopped.

Because the pies at Home Slice Pizza are all cooked to order directly on 2-inch stone, you'll have a little bit of time between placing your order and tasting your first bite of hot New York–style pizza; enjoy those garlic knots for starters, and your patience will be well rewarded.

Stroll down the street for another iconic Austin eatery.

THERE ARE LOTS OF FAMOUS MURALS ON SOUTH CONGRESS AVENUE.

Try to take a picture by these four:

"I Love You So Much," located on the side of Jo's Coffee, 1300 S. Congress Ave.

"Willie For President," located on the side of STAG, 100 E. Elizabeth St.

"Smile! Even If You Don't Want To," located directly across the street from the Willie For President mural, 1511 S. Congress Ave.

"Love From Austin," located on the side of Prima Dora, 1912 S. Congress Ave.

3

EXPERIENCE THE FAMOUS FLAGSHIP
LOCATION OF TORCHY'S TACOS

TORCHY'S TACOS is an absolute must-visit when you're exploring Austin's food scene. It started as a humble food trailer on South First in Bouldin Creek (this location no longer exists), and those "Damn Good Tacos" grew in popularity throughout the years. Now there are brick-and-mortar locations not only in Austin, but also all around Texas, Oklahoma, and Colorado. If you're going to choose just one location in Austin to try that famous Torchy's queso and a fried avocado taco, head to the flagship restaurant on South Congress. The building was designed to mimic iconic drive-in diners from the '50s with bold red "X" beams and a bright "TORCHY'S" marquee across the top of the building. On busy weekends, the line can extend out the front door, but the dining room and large pet-friendly patio provide plenty of seating.

Torchy's serves the whole menu all day, so you can order guacamole and chips at 7 am, or a Wrangler breakfast taco (scrambled eggs and potatoes with smoked beef brisket, jack cheese, and tomatillo sauce) at 10 pm. These bold, creative tacos don't fit into the category of traditional Mexican tacos. Torchy's has their own taco culture! Feeling crazy? Try the Independent, a flour tortilla full of battered and fried portobello mushroom strips, refried black beans, avocado, and ancho aioli. Feeling a little bit tame? The beef or chicken fajita taco is always available for folks who don't want anything too spicy or wild.

Regardless of the taco you order, the green chile queso topped with fresh guacamole, cotija cheese, cilantro, and Torchy's spicy diablo sauce is always the right choice. It's widely regarded as Austin's favorite queso, and it's instantly addicting.

Tacos are great at all hours of the day, but what's the beverage equivalent? Our next stop has #RoséAllDay!

4

GRAB YOUR GIRLFRIEND AND INDULGE IN FRIES AND ROSÉ AT JUNE'S ALL DAY

JUNE'S ALL DAY, which was on *Food & Wine's* 2017 Best New Restaurants list, is an adorable corner cafe that offers an all-day bistro menu. I love stopping by in the morning to enjoy a lazy cup of coffee and a croissant on the small outdoor patio, or making dinner reservations for a Sunday night double date with my husband and two of our friends. June's is easy and comfortable.

The daily happy hour is a beautiful time to stop by, perch at the counter, and order a rosy pink burger with shoestring fries and a glass of bubbly. The black-and-white tiles on the floor convey a classic, timeless elegance, and the marble countertops mean that every photo you take of the food will be Insta-worthy.

If happy hour isn't your thing, the "all day" in the title means that you can stop in at all hours of the day to indulge. Breakfast and brunch are served daily with lovely items like a Farm Egg Omelet with Boursin, salted radish, and green salad, or a beautiful croque madame that will make you feel like you're in a French cafe. The menu extends from lunch into the late hours of the night with delectable entrees. Try the popular bone marrow Bolognese, a cozy dish with handkerchief pasta, kale, and salty parm, or the matzo ball caldo, a comforting soup made with poached chicken, veggies, and jalapeños.

The counter bar is a charming oasis of calm amid the bustle on SoCo. Step inside to escape the Austin heat, set your shopping bags down for a rest, and ask your server what the sommelier has recently put on the wine menu. Cheers to the good life!

Next up: an adorable place to enjoy both food and people-watching on South Congress.

5 SNACK ON TOKYO-INSPIRED STREET FOOD AT LUCKY ROBOT

Bright lights, fun neon colors, fish that has been imported from renowned Tsukiji Fish Market in Tokyo, and farm-to-table produce: LUCKY ROBOT brings Tokyo street food to the heart of Austin.

Sit on indoor swings (yes, swings) and order hot or cool apps, bowls, sushi and sashimi, maki rolls, and a beautiful selection from the daily market fish, flown in from Japan and around the world.

Sustainability is an important component to Lucky Robot's menu. They recognize that resources are limited, and humanity hasn't done the best job at treating our oceans with respect. Lucky Robot does their part to source sustainably. They recently featured a monthlong campaign called #timeoutfortuna, clearing tuna from menu one day per week to bring awareness to the fact that bluefin tuna is one of the most overfished sushi items and needs to be protected.

Lucky for you: there are many types of delectable (and safe!) fish to enjoy on the menu. The Chiki Toro is a signature *nigiri* made with Hawaiian bigeye tuna and house-cured lardo. It mimics the deep flavor of *otoro* (or "fatty tuna") with a sustainable version.

Try the hand-pressed pork and shrimp dumplings with cranberry nimono, a semi-sweet sauce, the sweet, crispy Brussels sprouts with lemongrass soy, and a *nomnomiyaki* cabbage and pork belly pancake with crispy shallots, spicy mayo, and a sunny-side-up egg. And be sure to ask your server about the most exciting fish to try that day.

Wine has long enjoyed being a topic of education and discussion, and craft cocktail bars and microbreweries have earned quite the media buzz

LEARN MORE ABOUT SAKE FROM LORA BLACKWELL, LUCKY ROBOT'S OWN SAKE SOMMELIER

Nama sake is growing in popularity. *Nama* is unpasteurized and contains active enzymes that give a wonderful youthful, lively taste!

Sake is a source of umami, a natural flavor enhancer, also found in Parmesan, mushrooms, and tomatoes.

I love the broad scope of flavors found in sake. Tasting notes for our sake list range from butter to bananas Foster, from fresh mushroom to ripe cantaloupe.

There's a misconception that only cheap sake should be served warm. Warmed sake expresses aromas, tastes, and textures that are suppressed when served chilled.

The yeast used in sake production has an incredible impact on the aroma of sake. Yeast #9 is one of the most commonly used for highly aromatic ginjo and daiginjo sakes.

in recent years, but sake is still an under-represented beverage in most United States cities. Lucky Robot recognized that and quickly became one of the best places in Austin to learn about sake by hiring their own sake sommelier. Order a flight of sake and enjoy tasting the subtle nuances.

Lucky Robot is next to Amy's Ice Creams. I try to save just a little bit of room so that I can head there for a scoop after dinner.

6

MAKE YOUR INNER CHILD HAPPY WITH A DOUBLE (OR TRIPLE) SCOOP AT AMY'S ICE CREAMS

I can tell you from experience that ice cream is a great way to endure the blistering Texas summers. Two or three scoops of ice cream, piled high and melting off a sweet vanilla waffle cone, have helped me make my way through decades of triple-digit summer temperatures. And if you're on SoCo and need a cool treat, **AMY'S ICE CREAMS** is your best bet.

Amy's has been Austin's most popular ice cream shop since 1984. There are locations all over town, but the South Congress walk-up window is still my favorite. It's just a few blocks away from the South Congress Bridge, where rows of people line up to watch the Mexican free-tailed bats emerge from the hiding place under the bridge every night from March to October. When I have guests in town, one of my favorite summer activities is to grab a scoop at Amy's (I love ordering Mexican vanilla with cookie dough and rainbow sprinkles) and walk a few blocks north to watch the bats.

Amy's has more than 350 rotating flavors . . . think you can try them all? Several flavors are always on the menu, like Mexican vanilla, sweet cream, and dark chocolate. The crazier flavors come and go, so I try to taste them while they're around; I love the spicy chipotle chocolate mixed with salted whiskey caramel, and Zilker mint chip. Once you eventually choose a flavor, you also have the option of adding crush'ns and toppings like pecans, oatmeal cookies, or marshmallows for thousands of flavor combinations.

After a long day of browsing the shops of South Congress, you'll be ready to unwind and savor a slow dinner at out next stop: Perla's.

7

DRESS UP FOR DATE NIGHT AT PERLA'S, THE FINEST SEAFOOD RESTAURANT IN AUSTIN

I can think of no better way to finish up a day on SoCo than with a glorious evening spent at **PERLA'S**. This seafood restaurant is the epitome of what Austin, Texas, considers an "upscale" restaurant, which is to say . . . it's still very casual. The Gulf Coast–inspired seafood dishes are exceptional, the raw bar is among the best in the city, and the attentive staff is friendly and knowledgeable. But this is still Austin, Texas, and we love to wear jeans and sundresses and sandals. The McGuire-Moorman Hospitality group has managed to create a special occasion restaurant that's still casual enough for Austin.

Perhaps it's because of the bright, twinkly lights on the patio, the crisp, white tablecloths, or the icy trays of raw oysters being scurried around the room, but there's a definite spirit of elegance and celebration in the air.

Although fresh fish and oysters are flown in daily from both East and West Coasts, Gulf Coast seafood is emphasized. Start with the cornmeal-fried oysters with Chili Morita and slaw for the table, and try the crispy Texas Gulf snapper for a true taste of Texas's best seafood.

South Congress Austin

The oak-shaded outdoor patio, which faces South Congress Avenue, absorbs the energy from the lively tourist street. I think fondly of many happy evenings I've spent sipping coastal cocktails on Perla's giant patio with family and close friends.

THE CESAR CHAVEZ CRAWL

1. Fuel your weekend with a hearty ranch-to-table brunch at JACOBY'S RESTAURANT AND MERCANTILE, 3235 E. CESAR CHAVEZ ST., AUSTIN, (512) 366-5808, JACOBYSAUSTIN.COM

2. Treat yourself to scratch-made vegan sweets at CAPITAL CITY BAKERY, 2211 E. CESAR CHAVEZ ST., AUSTIN, (512) 666-7427, SHOPCAPITALCITYBAKERY.COM

3. Relax with tacos and lattes at CENOTE, 1010 E. CESAR CHAVEZ ST., AUSTIN, (512) 524-1311, CENOTEAUSTIN.COM

4. Eat award-winning food in a renovated laundromat at LAUNDERETTE, 2115 HOLLY ST., AUSTIN, (512) 382-1599, LAUNDERETTEAUSTIN.COM

5. Pretend you're in Italy with Neapolitan-style pies at BUFALINA, 1519 E. CESAR CHAVEZ ST., AUSTIN, (512) 524-2523, BUFALINAPIZZA.COM

6. Sip all the sour beer at BLUE OWL BREWING, 2400 E. CESAR CHAVEZ ST. #300, AUSTIN, (512) 593-1262, BLUEOWLBREWING.COM

7. Sneak away to a sultry date night at JUSTINE'S BRASSERIE, 4710 E. 5TH ST., AUSTIN, (512) 385-2900, JUSTINES1937.COM

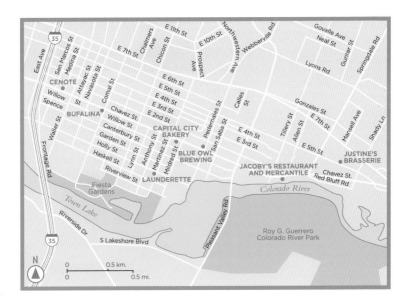

Cesar Chavez

Tacos, Beer, and Funky Patios

CESAR CHAVEZ, A SMALL EAST AUSTIN NEIGHBORHOOD NAMED after the American civil rights activist, has experienced rapid growth in the past decade. It's one of Austin's oldest neighborhoods, and now one of the hottest areas to live, eat, and hang out in Austin. Although it's just a few blocks from downtown, Cesar Chavez still has a neighborhood vibe, making this a popular place for locals to live and visitors to stay in boutique hotels or Airbnbs. And since the area is still very residential, you're going to have a lot of fun walking your way through this day of eating. As the population density has increased, so have the restaurant choices. Sure, Cesar Chavez is still a great place to find the Austin classics, like taco shops, dive bars, and barbecue food trucks. But the area also includes farm-to-table fare, trendy pizzerias, and restaurants from award-winning chefs. I've listed seven of the best options for eating and drinking your way down Cesar Chavez, but rest assured that there are many other fun neighborhood gems that you might stumble upon as you explore. Get your eating pants ready!

1

FUEL YOUR WEEKEND WITH A HEARTY RANCH-TO-TABLE BRUNCH AT JACOBY'S RESTAURANT AND MERCANTILE

JACOBY'S ranch-to-table, family-owned restaurant is just about as "Texas" of a dining experience as you can find. What started as a Feed and Seed in 1981 has grown into a vertically integrated business. Here's what that means: You're sitting at the darling Jacoby's Restaurant and Mercantile in east Austin, eating a juicy cheeseburger, which was made with Jacoby's beef, from an animal raised on Jacoby's ranch, which was fed Jacoby's own specially mixed finishing ration, which was made by Jacoby's Feed and Seed. No need to question how the meat was raised or sourced! The cheeseburger at Jacoby's is one of the best in town, and the duck confit migas is a feast of tender strips of duck breast, queso, ranchero, sour cream, scrambled eggs, crunchy house chips, and pico. Another crowd favorite, the chicken-fried steak and waffles, is covered in homemade sausage gravy and maple syrup, because this is brunch, my friend, and there's no need to skimp.

Of course, there are plenty of menu items for folks who aren't interested in meat. Head to the "SWEET" section of the menu for a list of breads, cakes, and scones, all made by the resident pastry chef. The sweets menu is constantly rotating, except for one constant item: Grandma Hager's strawberry cake. There is something so classically Southern about a thick slice of light pink cake covered with a layer of strawberry frosting. The most recent time I brunched here, I ordered a gooey cinnamon roll to share with the table. Needless to say, I immediately regretted not getting my own. The pimento grits with BBQ  butter and pickled red pepper are, however, a nice menu item to share with friends. They're rich and cheesy, perfect for sneaking in small bites to accompany your entree of choice. And the maple pecan pancakes, topped with whipped cream and maple syrup, are a hearty, decadent option for an entree or a shareable plate. Bacon is listed as an option for the pancakes, but is it really an option? As we've already established: Brunch is not a time to cut corners.

A food crawl is all about variety, and now that you've eaten a carnivorous brunch, make a 180-degree turn and head to a vegan bakery.

2

TREAT YOURSELF TO SCRATCH-MADE VEGAN SWEETS AT CAPITAL CITY BAKERY

Kindness is key at CAPITAL CITY BAKERY. Everything at this vegan, woman-owned bakery is made from scratch with lots of love, but there's so much more to this place that makes it special.

It started as a food truck, but, as with most excellent food trucks, the team outgrew their space and opened a storefront on East Cesar Chavez in what used to be a single-family home. Everything they make is ridiculously tasty, but here are a few suggestions to get you started.

The strawberry pop tarts sell out quickly, so if you see any left, grab one! The flaky crust is filled with a thick, sweet strawberry center and covered in white icing and rainbow sprinkles. It will take you back to your childhood!

Cupcakes are the number-one seller here. There are several rotating flavors each week, but if you're only going to try one, go for the confetti. Their white cake recipe took years to perfect, but one bite will tell you that all the recipe testing was worth it. The soft mound of vanilla frosting on top is the perfect vegan dupe for buttercream.

Capital City Bakery does custom cakes! They offer everything from classic three-tier wedding cakes to quirky themed birthday cakes.

If you want to scroll through some serious #foodporn, look at their Instagram account (@capcitybakery). Whether you choose to enjoy your treat at the adorable bungalow cafe, or take it to go on your food crawl through Cesar Chavez, rest assured that everything here is vegan, cholesterol-free, and made with local ingredients when possible. And, most importantly, it's all completely scrumptious.

The next stop on this food crawl is a place to recharge and get some caffeine!

3

RELAX WITH TACOS AND LATTES AT CENOTE

If the Cesar Chavez neighborhood had a poster child, it would probably be **CENOTE.** This is a quirky little hangout spot where you can enjoy coffee and homemade breakfast tacos in the morning, beers and burgers in the afternoon, or a bottle of wine in the evening, all in a renovated historic house from 1887. The interior is painted a calming shade of blue, and tables are scattered around the room for couples on coffee dates or solo laptop workers. The full menu is sourced responsibly, using pasture-raised eggs, and local, hormone-free produce. Breakfast tacos are served on Cenote's very own 50/50 corn and flour tortillas; they have the soft texture of flour tortillas, but the gritty flavor of corn. Stopping by for lunch? Try the ⅓-pound Texas beef burger, or the house-made veggie burger with beans and beets from

WHO WAS CESAR CHAVEZ?

American labor leader and civil rights activist who devoted his life to improving working conditions and pay for farm workers.

Lived from 1927 to 1993.

Cofounded the United Farm Workers of America with Dolores Huerta.

Coined the phrase *si, se puede!* (Yes, you can!)

Used nonviolent means, like marches and hunger strikes, to direct attention to farm workers.

local farm Johnson's Backyard Garden.

Winter weather doesn't last long in Austin, but I love to order the chai latte when a cold front comes through town. It's a warm and cozy drink that's made from scratch in Cenote's kitchen.

Step out to the front patio, and you might stumble upon your next favorite singer/songwriter singing on the small corner stage. But my favorite place to hunker down at Cenote is the small side patio, adjacent to Medina Street. This little hideaway feels like a secret garden. It's surrounded by a shady canopy of greenery and kept cool with several fans.

Regardless of what you order or where you choose to relax, Cenote provides a darling place to enjoy a drink and rest your feet before continuing your Cesar Chavez food crawl.

4

EAT AWARD-WINNING FOOD IN A RENOVATED LAUNDROMAT AT LAUNDERETTE

LAUNDERETTE is worth every bit of hype it has received. You might have heard of this restaurant from *Food & Wine* (2016 Best Restaurants of the Year), *Texas Monthly* (2016 Best New Restaurants in Texas), or because of its James Beard Foundation Award nominations. This little New American restaurant is in one of the most unusual restaurant buildings in Austin: a renovated laundromat and gas station. The interior is sleek and trendy, and the large patio makes a lovely place to enjoy cocktails with a group of pals. Plates here are meant to be shared; Chef Rene Ortiz has created a fun mix of cultures with his snacky starters, show-stopping vegetable plates, and wood-grilled entrees. Menu items are rotating, but plan on starting with a few small bites

for the table. I love the bright beet hummus with *labneh* or the homemade potato chips and pimento cheese. The crab and avocado toast on semolina bread is heaped high with bold flavors; there is no shame in ordering toast for dinner when it tastes this good. The brick chicken, served on a bed of sauce aligot and braised greens, is a must-try item. Don't be fooled by the simple name; this piece of tender chicken in a flavorful, crisp crust is a showstopper and crowd favorite.

Pastry chef Laura Sawicki's desserts shouldn't be considered an afterthought. Some people come to Launderette for desserts alone! The birthday cake ice cream sandwich is an iconic Launderette menu item that tastes just as good as it looks on Instagram. Imaginative icebox pies, semifreddos, cakes, and sorbets are prepared with Chef Laura's delicate balance of flavor and elaborate plating skills. I once made the mistake of leaving Launderette without ordering dessert, and that will never happen again.

5

PRETEND YOU'RE IN ITALY WITH NEAPOLITAN-STYLE PIES AT BUFALINA

If you're in search for some seriously delicious Neapolitan pizza in Austin, Texas, look no further than BUFALINA. This teeny east Cesar Chavez restaurant doesn't take reservations and only holds about 40 people, which means that there's always a line on the weekends. If you show up and there's a wait in front of you, try to squeeze your way to the bar and order a cocktail to sip while you wait for a table.

The star of the room is a large, white pizza oven imported from Naples, which heats upwards of 900 degrees Fahrenheit, cooking each pie for 90 seconds or so. The result? A thin, flat pizza with a puffy, chewy crust, and a hot, cheesy center topped with fresh ingredients. These pizzas are no joke.

If you're a bit of a purist about your Neapolitan pizza styles and you want something classic, go with the Margherita. It's topped with a simple scattering of tomato, mozzarella, basil, and Parm, and it is perfection. And you can't go wrong with any of the fun variations they have with other toppings. I never get tired of the roasted mushroom with fontina and lemon ricotta!

The wine list at Bufalina is exactly what you would expect from a serious Italian pizzeria. The menu boasts an extensive list of Italian wines to be paired with your 12-inch Calabrese pizza. Order by the glass or by the bottle, and enjoy sips of wine with your decadent pizza feast. When you finish that wine bottle, walk down the street to a fun little spot for sour beer.

6

SIP ALL THE SOUR BEER AT
BLUE OWL BREWING

BLUE OWL BREWING is a small corner brewery on Cesar Chavez and Pedernales. It's a sweet spot to gather for an afternoon or evening of beer tasting. I love this place because it is so different from what most breweries in Austin are doing: Blue Owl uses sour-mashing to brew tart versions of beer styles that you already know and love.

What is sour-mashing? Head brewer Jeff Young describes it as this: "The essence of sour-mashing is using the naturally occurring wild bacteria from malted barley to produce acidity (sourness) in the wort. That

sourness carries on to the finished beer for a balanced, clean, and zippy tart component."

Maybe you're new to sour beer? Start with the Little Boss tart wheat beer. It's not too complex, just a nice, clean flavor for sour newbies. I personally love this one on the hottest days of the year. If you're already a sour-beer nerd and are looking for something unique, try the taproom exclusives, which are experimental limited batches, usually with only one or two kegs. This is where Jeff plays around with his beer to create new variations, and he's come up with some fun flavor combinations like the Professor Black (sour cherry stout) with coffee, or the Czech Czech (sour Czech pilsner) with crunch berries. This is definitely not your typical brewery experience. Get ready to taste lots of fun and funky flavors, and enjoy chatting with your bartender to learn more about the beer!

The good eats and drinks extend late into the night just down the road at Justine's Brasserie.

7

SNEAK AWAY TO A SULTRY DATE NIGHT AT JUSTINE'S BRASSERIE

Moody, sultry, oh-so-sexy, JUSTINE'S BRASSERIE is a French kitchen that's tucked far enough away on Cesar Chavez to be a decent drive from the rush of the town. The only clue you have that you're in the right place is the flashing neon sign facing the sidewalk; the rest of the restaurant is hidden behind a tall wall of greenery. Reservations aren't accepted here, so you'll probably be spending some time at the bar while you wait for a table.

Order a French 75 and a cheese board, and enjoy the jazz music and the sound of glasses clinking.

The kitchen stays open until 1:30 am, so plan on stopping here for a late-night bite. The French onion soup is a decadent starter, made with a homemade stock, sweet, caramelized onions, and covered in a thick layer of melted cheese. The classic French entrees are beautifully prepared. I love to order the *moules frites* paired with an elegant Chablis. The steamed mussels are served with delicate *pommes frites*, but you'll probably want to use some of the crusty French bread to soak up the buttery sauce. Another crowd favorite is the classic steak *frites*; enjoy the rosy pink rib eye and fries with your choice of sauce au poivre, tangy Roquefort sauce, or the classic beurre maitre d'. There is no wrong choice here; Justine's is a restaurant that relies just as heavily on the seductive ambience as it does on the excellent food and drinks. Raise your glass of deep-red Bordeaux, breathe in the night air, and cozy up to your date.

THE EAST AUSTIN CRAWL

1. Start your day with a cappuccino at hipster coffee shop **FLEET COFFEE**, 2427 WEBBERVILLE RD., AUSTIN, (512) 212-7174, FLEETCOFFEE.COM

2. Cameras ready for brunch at the adorable **HILLSIDE FARMACY**, 1209 E. 11TH ST., AUSTIN, (512) 628-0168, HILLSIDEFARMACY.COM

3. Escape to Argentina at **BUENOS AIRES CAFÉ**, 1201 E. 6TH ST., AUSTIN, (512) 382-1189, BUENOSAIRESCAFE.COM

4. Experience all the good vibes with beer and tacos at **LAZARUS BREWING COMPANY**, 1902 E. 6TH ST., AUSTIN, (512) 394-7620, LAZARUSBREWING.COM

5. Eat locally, the Texas way, at **DAI DUE**, 2406 MANOR RD., AUSTIN, (512) 524-0688, DAIDUE.COM

6. Sip on boozy milkshakes at **PROHIBITION CREAMERY**, 1407 E. 7TH ST., AUSTIN, (512) 992-1449, PROHIBITIONCREAMERY.COM

7. Corn is the star at **SUERTE**, 1800 E. 6TH ST., AUSTIN, (512) 953-0092, SUERTEATX.COM

8. Sneak away to cocktails in a secret garden at **AH SING DEN**, 1100 E. 6TH ST., AUSTIN, (512) 467-4280, AHSINGDEN.COM

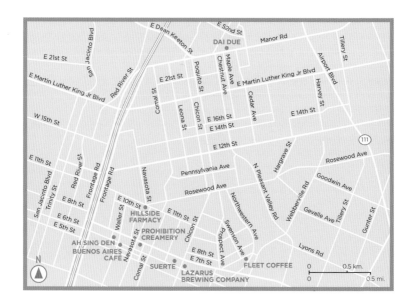

East Austin

Doing Our Best to Keep Austin Weird

OUR FOOD CRAWL CONTINUES JUST A FEW BLOCKS NORTH OF Cesar Chavez into East Austin. This is an all-encompassing title that I'm using to describe several small neighborhoods that all come together to create one big, food-dense region.

East Austin has experienced more gentrification in the past decade than any other area of Austin. For a while, it was a low-income area of Austin. But proximity to downtown, among other reasons, has made it a trendy, expensive place to live with lots of mixed-use high-rise developments being built. With so many folks buying condos in east Austin, this is also a very popular place to open a restaurant.

If I had to choose a food theme for east Austin, it would be farm-to-table. East Austin happens to be home to several great farms, and the restaurants in this area can source locally . . . meaning, right down the street! Johnson's Backyard Garden, Boggy Creek Farm, and Green Gate Farms are just a few of the farms in east Austin.

There are many old-school Austin places still open, and I'll mention several of those. But there are also lots of fun, new, Insta-worthy hot spots that are worth a stop on your food crawl.

1

START YOUR DAY WITH A CAPPUCCINO AT HIPSTER COFFEE SHOP FLEET COFFEE

A perfect day begins with a perfect cup of coffee. FLEET is the most hipster; it takes pride in serving carefully prepared pour-overs, cappuccinos, and lattes in their small, triangular east Austin shop.

Lorenzo Perkins and Patrick Pierce opened this coffee shop after years of experience in Austin's best coffee shops. They've both won multiple awards at barista championships. They are, in a nutshell, the textbook example of "coffee nerds" and they chose to team up and open their own shop in a 364-square-foot corner of Webberville Road. The result? A perfectly comfortable, albeit tiny, place to perch for a moment and enjoy a pour-over and breakfast taco before starting your day.

The coffee is sourced from some of the world's most reputable coffee roasters, like 49th Parallel Coffee Roasters in Vancouver, Olympia Coffee Roasting Company in Washington, and Mad Cap Coffee Company in Grand Rapids. This shop is an excellent place to buy your own bag of beans to brew at home. The staff is friendly and always generous with their time when I have questions about the various roasts that are available to purchase.

Fleet has recognizable bright blue cups, which make every one of their beautifully prepared coffee drinks completely photo-worthy.

Be sure to take a picture of that #dailycortado and post it to Instagram before heading off to brunch!

TIP

Coffee and a blueberry muffin? Nope! Austin is all about coffee and breakfast tacos! Most coffee shops here will have a few breakfast tacos on the menu. They're either made in the coffee shop, or catered in each morning from Tacodeli or Veracruz, two local taco shop chains.

2 CAMERAS READY FOR BRUNCH AT THE ADORABLE HILLSIDE FARMACY

The population surge in east Austin has forced restaurant developers to be creative in finding places to call home. The HILLSIDE FARMACY team decided to take an old, crumbling building that used to house Hillside Drugstore and restore and repurpose it into the most darling little cafe. This is an all-day eatery with a bright, vibrant feel and a combination of healthy and indulgent eats. The checkered patio awning, vintage tile floor, and wallpapered walls instill an old-time soda fountain feel, but rest assured that the all-American menu, created by Chef Sonya Coté, makes this adorable eatery more than just an Instagrammable spot. The food absolutely could stand on its own, even if this weren't such a darn cute little place full of so much ambience. The charcuterie, homemade snacks and sandwiches, and raw bar make this a tasty choice for any time of day. For first-timers, though, breakfast is the sweetest time to stop by.

Try the pancakes, which are made thick and fluffy and full of loads of blueberries and a little

pop of citrus with an orange slice on top. Or for those who aren't interested in sugar for breakfast, the Smokey Denmark bangers and eggs is a feast with two sausages, scrambled local farm eggs, caramelized onions, tomato relish, and a chewy baguette. Whatever you order, enjoy the buzz of energy from dining at one of east Austin's most popular brunch spots.

Next up: another classic east Austin eatery, but this time with Argentine food!

3

ESCAPE TO ARGENTINA AT
BUENOS AIRES CAFÉ

The front door of this buzzing Argentine cafe is constantly opening and closing with smiling customers who know and love chef Reina and her daughter, Paola, who have been running this family business since the early 2000s. Reina, who was born and raised in Argentina, could only be asked to make her empanadas so many times before deciding to open her own little cafe. Opening a business as a female entrepreneur wasn't easy; Reina was turned down many times by potential lenders and landlords who didn't believe she would succeed. But perseverance paid off, and now Reina is the owner not only of this east side cafe, but also another location in west Austin.

The empanadas are a great place to start. Order the *carne picante*, full of spicy ground beef, green onions, raisins, green olives, and fresh herbs and spices, and enjoy that soft, flaky crust crumbling with every bite. Buenos Aires Cafe imports their oregano from Argentina to make the *provoleta*, a traditional Argentine charred provolone; Instagram that #cheesepull before scooping up the delicious melty dish onto crispy little pieces of bread.

Grilled meat is classic Argentine food; if you're only going to taste one thing from the grilled section of the menu, try the *parrillada*, which is a massive Argentine-style mixed grill of beef short ribs, chicken breast, and Chef Reina's house-made chorizo bratwurst.

Dessert is not to be missed here! The Dark and Spicy Crème Brûlée is an indulgent dark chocolate custard with spicy *pasilla*, cayenne peppers, and a few bright strawberries to counter the heat, or the lemon pie, made from Chef Reina's old family recipe.

After enjoying an Argentine feast, bring it back to Austin to enjoy something we do best: tacos and beer.

4 EXPERIENCE ALL THE GOOD VIBES WITH BEER AND TACOS AT LAZARUS BREWING COMPANY

Bright colors and bold beers are the theme of this multifunctional brewery/coffee shop/taco kitchen. LAZARUS BREWING COMPANY does a little bit of everything! The first thing you'll probably notice when you walk in is the mosaic disco antlers on the wall and the cozy leather couch underneath it. This is an eclectic assortment of decorations, but it makes for a fun place to bring a laptop and get some work done, or simply lounge with a couple friends on the weekend. Lazarus is a true neighborhood bar where locals show up day after day to get some of the best brews and tacos in town.

If you're new around here, try the Amandus Strong Belgian Golden Ale, a malty, medium-bodied beer that pairs perfectly with a bowls of warm chips and salsa. It won a gold medal at the 2017 Great American Beer Fest, an impressive feat to say the least. Or grab a flight of beer and try a sample of all of them! Lazarus brews styles from around the world. They have a French *saison*, a German Pilsner, and an American IPA. They're all great options for enjoying with some tacos on the patio.

The tacos here are no joke, either. Owner Christian Cryder wanted to create a food menu that had a simple offering of tacos, so that it feels like you're ordering from your favorite street-food cart. The emphasis is

on quality over quantity, because even though the menu is small, these pastor tacos rival the best in Austin. Be sure to place an order of *fundido* for the table, and grab some chips and guac while you're at it. The tortilla chips are delivered to your table hot, greasy, and salty.

After you've enjoyed some brews and good times with friends, head over to dinner at Dai Due.

5 EAT LOCALLY, THE TEXAS WAY, AT DAI DUE

The restaurant name says it all: DAI DUE comes from the Latin phrase "from the two kingdoms of nature, choose food with care." Chef Jesse Griffiths is all about carefully sourcing local Texas meat and produce that has been grown fairly and safely, supporting the local ranchers and farmers, and, of course, creating a hearty and mouthwatering menu of choices for hungry customers.

Dai Due started as supper club and a booth at the farmers market, and gradually grew into its own brick-and-mortar, with a downtown offshoot just a few miles away. Everything here is as local as possible. Chef Jesse is passionate about using Texas game on his menu. He even goes so far as to organize hunting trips through his New School of Traditional Cookery. Customers can purchase a class to learn how to shoot, clean, and cook their own game, and the day ends with a multicourse meal from the items covered in the class.

However, for many of us, we just want an exceptional dining experience, no hunting required. The beautiful east side restaurant is also a bakery and a butcher shop, so when you walk in, you'll see bakers kneading dough and you might even see a whole hog being wheeled on the ceiling track to the back kitchen.

The menu is constantly evolving, so I can't offer too many suggestions and guarantee they'll be there when you dine. But since the bread is being made right in front of your eyes, grilled mesquite sourdough with Fresno chile–whipped lard is a delicious place to start. The Supper Club menu is prix-fixe; it's fun to order with a group of people, then select the Texas wine you'd like to pair with it.

Dai Due has elevated the cuisine in Austin by not just sourcing from farm to table, but truly sourcing game that is native to Texas. Don't be scared off by chicken hearts or ground wild boar. This food is true Texas dining, and it's all delicious.

On your way out the door, stop by the butcher shop to purchase some grass-fed beef, free-roaming venison, or feral hog to cook at home. You'll have trouble finding another butcher shop in Austin that puts quite so much care into providing local and sustainably raised meat to their customers.

I hope you saved room for the next stop: a boozy milkshake at Prohibition Creamery!

6

SIP ON BOOZY MILKSHAKES AT PROHIBITION CREAMERY

Boozy milkshakes galore! PROHIBITION CREAMERY takes two things we all love (ice cream and bourbon) and mixes them together to create their classic boozy ice cream flavors. Mix and match flavors and toppings to try scrumptious scoops, shakes, floats, and malts. I love the signature bourbon, of course. It's the best-selling boozy flavor, and it evokes memories of eggnog-filled Christmas days spent by the fireplace. And the boozy milkshakes pack a punch with the addition of rich, creamy liquors like Bailey's and Rumchata. The Irish coffee milkshake is a little naughty and a little nice: both Bailey's and Chameleon Cold Brew coffee are blended into the creamy drink. As long as you're indulging in dessert and booze, why not add a little caffeine, too?

For youngsters or those who aren't interested in intoxicating themselves with anything other than sugar, the nonalcoholic flavors like cookie dough or cheesecake with graham swirl provide a merry little stop during your east Austin food crawl.

7. CORN IS THE STAR AT SUERTE

Sam Hellman-Mass, one of the cofounders of Odd Duck (see page 17 for more on Odd Duck) geeked out on all things corn before opening this award-winning restaurant. He traveled to Mexico, studied corn, figured out how to soak it and grind it and transform it into the most delectable corn tortillas you can possibly try, and then he created a restaurant all about corn. Say hello to SUERTE.

The word means "luck" in Spanish, and you're going to feel all that good fortune that you stumbled into this restaurant. The adorable pink door is a preview of the lovely design aesthetic that you'll see inside. Almost everything in the restaurant was designed with textiles from Mexico and Texas, like the tequila bottle chandeliers, the Texas pecan wood used to make the tables, and the beautiful pink-striped fabric that lines the chairs.

This is a place to order a tequila- or mezcal-based cocktail, because they have a great selection of

> "Making the masa and serving every tortilla warm from the first time it's cooked is the foundation of our cooking. The corn from Richardson Farms and Barton Springs Mill has a truly amazing flavor and Texas terroir."
>
> —Sam Hellman-Mass, owner of Suerte

those liquors. The bartender will help you find something fun and new to try on the cocktail menu .

The food menu is meant to be shared, making this a great place to go on a double date. Order two or three plates per person and enjoy tasty ceviche, tacos, and tostadas, and slightly larger entrees. I adore Suerte, because they manage to take ingredients that don't tend to have mouth-watering properties (the entire restaurant is based on a dry seed from the grass family, after all) and turn it into a delectable treat. The beet tostadas, for instance, don't draw me in with their name, but crispy corn chips covered in smashed avocado, peanut-walnut yum yum sauce, and bright pink pickled onions are so completely satisfying that I've ordered them every time I dine here.

The night doesn't have to end here! Head over to Ah Sing Den for some beautiful cocktails.

8 SNEAK AWAY TO COCKTAIL IN A SECRET GARDEN AT AH SING DEN

AH SING DEN resides on East Sixth, the slightly elevated and classier cousin to downtown's "Dirty Sixth," where undergrads and bachelor parties will swarm to find cheap shots, dance clubs, and greasy slices of late-night pizza. Although East Sixth technically starts on Congress and moves east, when you hear a local say, "I'm going out on East Sixth tonight," she's talking about the bars and restaurants on the east side of I-35, not the downtown bar scene. I know; it's all a bit confusing.

Here's the simple thing to remember: Ah Sing Den, named after East London's most famous opium den, is a place to enjoy a cozy conversation and craft cocktails amidst the brightly decorated interior, or sneak away to the back patio and dine under swinging paper lanterns and the sound of running water. I always feel like I've discovered a secret garden when I slip away to the back patio.

Come for the cocktails, but stay for morsels as well. The drinks are grouped by "Old World, New World, Indies, and Far East," and the flavors in each cocktail reflect the region from which it's from. For instance, the Wayward Spring from the Far East menu is a concoction that includes *baijiu*, a Chinese grain spirit, *shochu*, a Japanese spirit from rice, barley, or sweet potato, and Szechuan peppercorn, which gives off a mouth-numbing feel.

The "New World" drinks have more recognizable ingredients, like rye, mezcal, and tequila. All are exciting and beautifully presented to your table.

Snacks like Goat Cheese Rangoons or octopus tartare are tasty tidbits to enjoy alongside your cocktails. It's also worth mentioning that this is a lovely place to enjoy brunch if you're more of a morning bird than a night owl.

THE CLARKSVILLE CRAWL

1. Start your day with a French press at **CAFFÈ MEDICI**, 1101 W. LYNN ST., AUSTIN, (512) 524-5409, CAFFEMEDICI.COM

2. Enjoy a posh lunch at **JOSEPHINE HOUSE**, 1601 WATERSTON AVE., AUSTIN, (512) 477-5584, JOSEPHINEOFAUSTIN.COM

3. Enjoy an all-you-can-eat chef's tasting menu at **CAFE JOSIE**, 1200B W. 6TH ST., AUSTIN, (512) 322-9226, CAFEJOSIE.COM

4. Raise your martini to happy hour at **CLARK'S OYSTER BAR**, 1200 W. 6TH ST., (512) 297-2525, CLARKSOYSTERBAR.COM

5. Sink your teeth into an award-winning diner burger at **COUNTER CAFE**, 626 N LAMAR BLVD., AUSTIN, (512) 708-8800, COUNTERCAFE.COM

6. Find delicious eats at all hours of day or night at **24 DINER**, 600 N. LAMAR BLVD., AUSTIN, (512) 472-5400

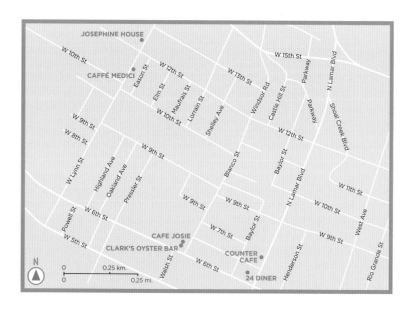

Clarksville

Stepping Back in Time

CLARKSVILLE IS A CHERISHED HISTORIC NEIGHBORHOOD; IT'S A little village of posh eateries, quaint coffee shops, and small houses from the early 1900s. It's the closest residential neighborhood to downtown Austin, so this is a fiercely competitive place to lock in real estate.

Clarksville dates back to 1871 and was named after its founder, freedman Charles Clark. It remains the oldest surviving freedom town west of the Mississippi. Sadly, Austin city policy pressured black communities to move east in the early 20th century, and Clarksville became increasingly hostile toward the original founding members. The streets weren't fully paved until the 1970s, when Clarksville was declared an official historic district. Thankfully, sums of money were provided to rehabilitate the houses and provide housing for various incomes, and fifth- or sixth-generation Clarksville residents still fight to keep the original houses and buildings of Clarksville standing. Now, Clarksville still has a neighborhood feel, despite its proximity to downtown. Spending a day in Clarksville is a little bit like stepping back in history to a simpler version of Austin. From a cozy coffee shop in a renovated house, to a posh and polished oyster bar, Clarksville offers a fun day of strolling and eating for anyone who is lucky enough to visit.

1

START YOUR DAY WITH A FRENCH PRESS AT CAFFÈ MEDICI

Austin's coffee scene is booming, but once upon a time, there weren't many options except for gas station coffee and a national megachain (you know the one . . .). CAFFÈ MEDICI is "Austin's original specialty coffee shop." They started talking about tasting notes, high-quality beans, and French presses before it was even cool.

There are now multiple locations in Austin, but the original Caffè Medici started on quiet little West Lynn Street in Clarksville. Walk up the creaky wooden stairs and enter a cozy ambience: The air smells like freshly brewed coffee, and the sound of clicking computer keys and chattering conversation make you feel like you're walking into a big, happy living room. I love meeting up with a friend or spending my morning here working on my laptop.

Caffè Medici offers the coffee you would expect to see in a specialty coffee shop: several single-origin options and all of the typical espresso drinks. There's always a fresh pot of coffee made from Wild Gift, a small-batch coffee roaster in Austin, and the espresso drinks are made with an espresso blend from Spyhouse Coffee Roasters in Minneapolis. Even with those two solid options, you might want to venture into the rotating roasters and try one of the single-origin options.

This is currently the largest Austin coffee chain; if your Clarksville food crawl doesn't allow time to stop by, you might be able to venture into one of the other Caffè Medici locations around the city. Each location has its own mood, but they're all buzzy, high-energy, comfortable places to grab a caffeinated beverage and a breakfast taco to start your day.

Clarksville Natural Grocery, a small, independent grocery store in the Clarksville neighborhood of Austin, joined forces with another small grocery store in Austin and became the first Whole Foods Market.

2 ENJOY A POSH LUNCH AT JOSEPHINE HOUSE

If you've figured out how to resist a darling breakfast spot, tell me your secret. I've yet to build any sort of resistance. I'm a sucker for the whitewashed walls, the renovated 1920s houses, the sunny front porches, and the wicker chairs. I want it all.

JOSEPHINE HOUSE doesn't rely on good looks alone, though. Breakfast, lunch, happy hour, and dinner are all sure to please the hungry customer. The lemon ricotta pancakes are some of the fluffiest you'll find in the whole city. They're served with blackberries, cultured butter, and a heavy pour of maple syrup, and they are scrumptious! If you're stopping by for lunch or dinner, the charcuterie board is one of the tastiest and most Instagrammable starters. And I can't get enough of the Josephine House burger and frites. Those crispy little fries are irresistible!

3

ENJOY AN ALL-YOU-CAN-EAT CHEF'S TASTING MENU AT CAFE JOSIE

Have you ever splurged on a chef's tasting menu, paid triple digits for your meal, and then walked away and thought, "I'm still hungry"? That won't happen at **CAFE JOSIE**. This is the first place in Austin where you can enjoy "The Experience," Austin's first and only unlimited chef's tasting menu. One fixed price will buy you as many small plates as you

can eat. Although this is an all-you-can-eat experience, you'll still enjoy beautifully plated seasonal fare that will wow your taste buds. Don't expect anything less.

The bar menu is made to complement the tasting menu. Explore wine from around the globe and right here in Texas hill country. The cocktails are highly approachable but offer unique twists on standard favorites: The Old Austin is Cafe Josie's Texas take on an old fashioned, but with added notes of pecan for a unique twist

As you work your way to the food menu, remember that, while it is all you can eat, the plates are fairly filling and unless you're Michael Phelps and consuming 12,000 calories a day, you might not be able to try everything on the menu. Start with the popular fried brussels sprouts, which are caramelized in Dijon rum glaze and served with rum-soaked cherries and candied pecans. They're sweet and could almost pass for dessert, but remember, these are brussels sprouts, so they're healthy. The shells and cheese with cheddar, smoked Gouda, and bacon onion jam is another favorite splurge-worthy starter. There are so many lovely options for main dishes: Beer-battered Gulf shrimp, grilled Gulf redfish with candied grapefruit

Want to check out another fun tasting menu in Austin? Head up north to **Barley Swine,** the sister restaurant of Odd Duck (Chapter 3) for a delicious meal of small plates!

and pomegranate, and braised baby back ribs with fish sauce caramel are just a few of the entrees you can expect to see on this feast of small plates.

Also worth noting: Show up to dinner a little bit early and enjoy happy hour prices on drinks and a discounted rate on The Experience. (Check the website for exact prices.)

Next up: ice cold martinis at one of Austin's favorite oyster bars!

5

RAISE YOUR MARTINI TO HAPPY HOUR AT CLARK'S OYSTER BAR

Oh, the charm! CLARK'S OYSTER BAR on West Sixth Street is a buzzing and bustling bar with all of the textile treats for a design-lover's dream. The interior is divided into three parts: a quaint bar area with round stools and a tall table for perching, a snug dining space with white tablecloths, and an outdoor patio with white and yellow striped umbrellas and cooling fans. This is a very popular place to enjoy ice-cold oysters and martinis in the summer. The entire restaurant has a beachy feel with nautical sea-green accents amid the bright-white tiles. It feels preppy and welcoming at the same time.

Enjoy your house-baked sourdough bread while you settle in and prepare to stay for a while; Clark's is made for lingering. Sip your Champagne, slurp a fresh oyster, and . . . was that your imagination, or did you just feel a sea breeze from Nantucket Bay? No, we're still in Austin. But the New England clam chowder will instantly transport you to a city that's not quite so landlocked.

Clark's is an oyster bar, but don't ignore the burger! It's a favorite in Austin. The Black Angus burger is pan-roasted and served with crunchy shoestring fries or a tangy slaw. Either option is delectable during a long and lazy lunch or happy hour.

Save room for one more burger at our next stop!

6

SINK YOUR TEETH INTO AN AWARD-WINNING DINER BURGER AT COUNTER CAFE

COUNTER CAFE is right between Clarksville and downtown. It's so small, it's hardly noticeable amid all the glitz of the new downtown high-rise condos, but this breakfast and lunch spot has an award-winning burger, one of the best breakfasts in town, and a loyal fan base.

Take your pick: one of the ten bar stools inside, or a two-top table pressed against the wall. This tiny diner provides what is only absolutely necessary: a long counter for food prep, a big, sizzling grill, tables for customers, and a narrow walkway for the busy waitstaff. If you manage to snag a bar stool, you'll be inches away from the food prep area (which is always my favorite place to dine; I love watching the food being prepared!).

The menu focuses on what is seasonal and local, but don't be mistaken: This is still classic, greasy diner food. The Counter Burger features a thick, grass-fed beef patty, which is cooked to order, topped with sharp cheddar cheese, and served on a pillowy-soft sourdough bun that has a subtle sweetness. This burger was mentioned as number two on the "50 Greatest Hamburgers in Texas" list by *Texas Monthly*. That's no small feat in this beef-loving state.

Both breakfast and lunch are served until 3 pm, which means choosing your menu item is extra difficult! Consider the crab cake Benedict, made with Counter Cafe's hearty biscuits and hand-made crab cakes, or the hot cake, which is, as the menu describes, literally as big as your plate.

Service only goes until 3 pm, so grab some breakfast or lunch before heading back out to explore Clarksville.

7

FIND DELICIOUS EATS AT ALL HOURS OF DAY OR NIGHT AT 24 DINER

There are several places in Austin that are good for all-night eats. The famous Magnolia Cafe is open 24 hours, and they're famous for their *queso* and for serving President Obama when he came through Austin. And then there's Kerbey Lane, which has multiple locations and the most popular pancakes in town. And then there's 24 DINER, which has a greasy spoon name but is anything but that.

Just as the name suggests, 24 Diner is open 24 hours a day. They offer local, organic food, a killer wine list, and healthy options as well as completely decadent brunch dishes. I love their big, bright salads with zingy house-made vinaigrettes when I'm craving some whole foods, but I also adore the yeast-risen Belgian waffles with fried chicken and brown sugar butter when the brunch craving hits.

This is an excellent place for weekend brunch and 3 am diner food, but don't forget about their dinner menu! Chef Andrew Curren has created a fantastic bunch of options to make this your next favorite dinner restaurant in Austin. The portions here are massive, so come hungry! The Sweet and Spicy Burger is a crowd favorite. The sweetness from the bacon and apple jam contrasting with the spicy relish will make your mouth do a little happy dance. All of the burgers and sandwiches are served with a heap of fresh-cut fries, hot and salty and ready to be devoured.

24 Diner is a gem in the Austin dining scene. It's unique because it's one of the few places that not only offers locally sourced food, but also offers it at any random hour of the day or night. Whether you've been out with friends drinking on Sixth Street, or you work a late night shift at your job, or you're just an exceptionally late night owl and need something to nosh on at 3 am, nothing in the world tastes as good as a plate of those hot and flavorful chili cheese fries when you're feeling particularly hungry.

THE DRAG CRAWL

1. Cozy up with French food and beer at HOPFIELDS, 3110 GUADALUPE ST., SUITE #400, AUSTIN, (512) 537-0467, HOPFIELDSAUSTIN.COM

2. Smell the baking bread at TEXAS FRENCH BREAD, 2900 RIO GRANDE ST., AUSTIN, (512)499-0544, TEXASFRENCHBREAD.COM

3. Step back in time to 1926 at DIRTY MARTIN'S PLACE, 2808 GUADALUPE ST., AUSTIN, (512) 477-3173, DIRTYMARTINS.COM

4. Craft your own *donburi* Japanese rice bowl at DON JAPANESE KITCHEN, 2716 GUADALUPE ST., AUSTIN, (281) 725-3686, FACEBOOK.COM/DONJAPANESE

5. Bite into a spicy Reuben at FRICANO'S DELI, 2405, NUECES ST., AUSTIN, (512) 482-3322, FRICANOSDELI.COM

6. Sip on margaritas at EL PATIO, one of Austin's oldest Tex-Mex restaurants, 2938 GUADALUPE ST., AUSTIN, (512) 476-5955, ELPATIOAUSTIN.COM

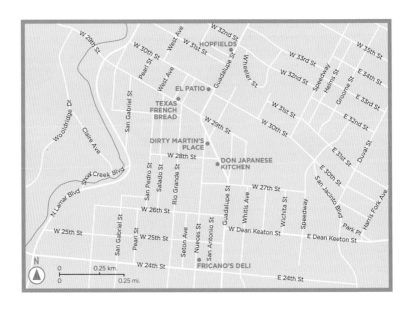

The Drag

Cheap Eats for Dorm-Dwellers

IF YOU FALL UNDER THE DEMOGRAPHIC OF 19-YEAR-OLD COLLEGE student with $8 cash in your wallet, this chapter is for you. Say hello to Austin's most student-friendly foodie area: The Drag.

Located on the western border of the University of Texas at Austin campus, The Drag is a 10-block stretch of Guadalupe Street that caters to UT students. This is where you can find dive bars, campus bookstores, funky fashion stores, and (most importantly for this book) cheap eats.

Walking along The Drag is a great way to spend a day food crawling through Austin, because there's a wide variety of ethnicities represented in the food here. And while "cheap eats" is the subtitle of this chapter, there are a few upscale eateries mixed in, too.

I adore eating lunch near campus for a couple of reasons. First, it brings me back to my days at the University of Texas. Eating out is slightly more fun now that I can afford both the drink and the chips with my sandwich without worrying about having any grocery money left. Secondly, I love eating on The Drag because it's in central Austin, which means some of the restaurants here have been around since the early 1900s.

Take Dirty Martin's Place, for instance. Walk into this little burger shack, and you'll see photos on the wall of what Austin looked like in 1930. Dirty Martin's is still in the original location it held back then, although what's around it has completely changed. The restaurant used to be in what was very far north Austin, but as Austin has grown and grown, it's now considered central.

Get ready to eat and drink your way through some of UT Austin's favorite restaurants from the past 90 years.

COZY UP WITH FRENCH FOOD AND BEER AT HOPFIELDS

Dark and cozy are the first two words that come to mind to describe this sweet little French spot by husband-wife team Bay and Lindsay Anthon. They serve approachable and uncomplicated French food, which one would typically expect to be paired with wine. But they went a little Austin on us (keeping things weird, for those of you who forgot the slogan . . .) and decided to specialize in craft beer instead of wine. That is one of the many things that make **HOPFIELDS** a unique spot to stop on your day of eating through Austin.

This is a fun place to visit solo, on a date, or with a group. Dining alone? Snag a seat at the small counter near the front door. You'll have a first-row seat to the rotating tap bar, and you can bug the bartender with all of your beer questions as you dive into that hearty Pascal Burger, a decadent patty topped with Camembert, cornichons, whole-grain mustard, and caramelized onions on a fluffy brioche bun. It's served with their famous *frites*

and house-made aioli. If you're here on a date, lucky you! This is a romantic place because there are several nooks and crannies where you can enjoy a quiet meal and conversation. There's also a back room available to rent for large groups who love to enjoy French food and craft beer.

If you're looking for a lovely weekend brunch, Hopfields has an extraordinary menu of classics like French toast, omelets, eggs Benedict, and a hearty full English breakfast. It's quite a lovely little spot to linger for a while.

2 SMELL THE BAKING BREAD AT TEXAS FRENCH BREAD

I adore a good bakery, and I also adore a family-run business, so it's no surprise that I'm obsessed with this sweet little neighborhood spot. And I'm not alone—Austin has been enjoying freshly baked breads and pastries and delicious homemade sandwiches and soups at **TEXAS FRENCH BREAD** since 1981.

Texas French Bread is a charming place to stop by on any morning of the week and order a table full of beautiful breakfast items. I can't get enough of those sweet almond croissants, cinnamon rolls, and blueberry Danish. If you're in a hurry, stop in and order a pastry and a cup of coffee at the counter and take it to go with you. If you have the time to linger, the weekday breakfast and weekend brunch are a happy way to start the day. The Challah French Toast is made with their own soft homemade challah bread, dipped in egg yolk and grilled, and dusted with a snowfall of powdered sugar; it's somehow not too eggy, just sweet enough, and so fluffy. I have dreams about this stuff. I typically choose sweet over savory for breakfast, and the banana walnut pancakes with Vermont maple syrup are another delicious start to the day.

Texas French Bread is much more than a breakfast restaurant, though. They started as a bakery and they remain one of Austin's busiest bakeries. They source to many restaurants in Austin, so don't be surprised if you see this name if you're ordering a sandwich at a different restaurant. On the weekends, Texas French Bread sells loaves of their freshly baked artisan bread at some of Austin's busiest farmers markets.

And so, my friend, even if you're not able to make a visit to the Guadalupe location of Texas French Bread, you're likely to find this scrumptious bread somewhere in the city.

After indulging in breakfast, walk a few steps around the corner to Dirty Martin's Place.

3 DIRTY MARTIN'S PLACE

No, it's not a "dirty" restaurant. Let's start by clearing that up right away. DIRTY MARTIN'S PLACE originally had dirt floors when it opened as an eight-stool drive-in back in 1926. The restaurant was paved in 1951, and things have changed. But the important stuff remains: They still make the same 100 percent Angus beef burgers and onion rings that they did nearly a century ago.

As the cost of living increases in Austin, many old institutions have closed their doors. Dirty Martin's Place stays relevant in all of the important ways, like acquiring a liquor license to cater to the pre-game UT football fans, while still keeping their old-school charm.

Be sure to try the hand-cut onion rings and fries, prepared fresh every day. This is a family-friendly place where everyone, young and old, will enjoy classic diner food like fried pickles, bacon cheeseburgers, and vanilla malts.

The walls are adorned with framed memorabilia, like the original menu from Dirty Martin's Place. The price of a hamburger in 1926? Twenty-five cents!

Next up: While you won't find anything for 25 cents, you'll still get a lot of bang for your buck at Don Japanese Kitchen.

> "Many of our customers have been coming to Dirty's since the 1930s and 1940s. It is an Austin and University of Texas tradition to come to Dirty Martin's. We are an Austin institution. We have many longtime employees who know the customers like they are family. We treat our employees like family."
>
> —Daniel Young, GM of Dirty Martin's Place

4

CRAFT YOUR OWN DONBURI JAPANESE RICE BOWL AT DON JAPANESE KITCHEN

If you're looking for cheap eats in Austin, you'll be hard pressed to find anything near campus that offers a better deal than **DON JAPANESE KITCHEN**. What was once a food truck near the University of Texas has grown into a full-fledged storefront with daily lines of hungry college students eager for a meal they can purchase that won't break the bank.

The ordering process is fairly simple: Walk into the small shop, order a bowl from the menu, then walk to the back of the restaurant to pick it up. You can place it in a plastic bag, provided near the condiments, or sit down at one of the long tables to enjoy your meal before rushing off to your next class.

The Don is the classic starter bowl. Choose panko-breaded fried pork or chicken, tempura eggplant, or fried fish fillet; the rest of the bowl is filled with white sticky rice and nori strips. There are plenty of protein choices, like teriyaki chicken, pork belly, or fatty tuna, and they're all relatively inexpensive and served in heaping portions.

The Don-Style Fries are a carb lover's dream come true: a big bowl of hot waffle fries drizzled with tangy teriyaki and tangy spicy mayo. The line can get pretty long during weekday lunch hours, but the friendly staff works hard to keep things moving along.

Let's keep this food crawl moving to another great spot for students.

5

BITE INTO A SPICY REUBEN AT FRICANO'S DELI

Every college campus needs a good deli, and FRICANO'S is that for University of Texas. This is a small, noisy, neighborhood deli with big sandwiches and big character.

Paul Fricano partnered with some of his Brooklyn friends and opened this place in 2006. He outgrew the original location and moved to the current spot in West Campus, but even with the extra space, this cozy sandwich shop is always busy at lunchtime. Right around 11 am, students and faculty members start to line up to get their regular orders of sandwiches, chips, and black and white cookies. They consider themselves a "New York/Chicago/Austin Deli," because that's where the three owners are from, and there's a little bit of influence from all three of those places. The hearty bread is made every day by Chuy Guevara at Mi Tradición Bakery, delivered fresh to Fricano's, and piled high with tasty ingredients right behind the counter. The Cajun turkey on sourdough is the most popular sandwich here, and for good reason: It's got a kick of spice from the Cajun seasoning, jalapeño spread, and pepperjack cheese, the sourdough bread is grilled to a crunch, and the cheese is warm and melty. Paul's Reuben—a feast of corned beef, sauerkraut, swiss cheese, and homemade Thousand Island dressing on rye bread—is another best seller.

TIP

Order the **Ainsworth** sandwich at Fricano's and leave it up to the masters to create a sandwich with the best ingredients of the day. This menu item was named after Chris Ainsworth, a UT student who stopped by every day for the first four years Fricano's was open and would just say, "make me something!"

If you and your friend order an Ainsworth on the same day, you'll get two completely unique creations.

6

SIP ON MARGARITAS AT EL PATIO, ONE OF AUSTIN'S OLDEST TEX-MEX RESTAURANTS

There's something so comforting and quaint about an old Austin institution like this one. EL PATIO has been family-owned in Austin since 1954. I recently found myself here in the middle of the day, enjoying a solo lunch at a small table. I started chatting with the man sitting at the table next to me, and he told me he's been eating at El Patio since the day they opened. When he walked to the front counter to pay his tab, he received hugs and greetings from the dedicated staff. This is the type of neighborhood spot where everyone knows one another, and it's pretty rare to find something so family-focused in the booming and busy city of Austin, Texas. Step into El Patio, and you'll feel like you're stepping back in time.

The Mexican food here is no frills. It's simple, cheap, and greasy food. Start with some chips and *queso*, then move on to a platter of chicken nachos served on homemade fried tortilla shells. This place is all about the nostalgia. You won't find fancy food at El Patio, but that doesn't matter because they've already won over the hearts of Austinites.

Start with the chicken, bean, and cheese nachos on El Patio's homemade shells. All of the nachos are served with jalapeños. The tacos are served open-face; if you want to add grated cheese, you'll have to ask for it specifically. Top your tacos with beef, chicken, *queso*, or whatever sounds delicious to you in the moment. You really can't go wrong, here. As I mentioned: We're not trying to be fancy here.

THE HYDE PARK CRAWL

1. Get your green juice fix at **JUICELAND**, 4500 DUVAL ST., AUSTIN, (512) 380-9046, JUICELAND.COM

2. Eat a vegetarian meal at **MOTHER'S CAFE**, 4215 DUVAL ST., AUSTIN, (512) 451-3994, MOTHERSCAFEAUSTIN.COM

3. Nosh on homemade pies and pastries at **QUACK'S 43RD STREET BAKERY**, 411 E. 43RD ST., AUSTIN, (512) 453-3399, QUACKSBAKERY.COM

4. Take a cheese tasting class at **ANTONELLI'S CHEESE SHOP**, 4220 DUVAL ST., AUSTIN, (512) 531-9610, ANTONELLISCHEESE.COM

5. Wine and dine at **VINO VINO**, 4119 GUADALUPE ST., AUSTIN, (512) 465-9282, VINOTX.COM

Hyde Park

Austin's First Suburb

IF YOU WALK THROUGH HYDE PARK TODAY, YOU'LL STILL SEE glimpses of what it originally built to be: an affluent suburb for Austin's upper class. The neighborhood used to be full of Queen Anne–style mansions and large, grassy estates lining the streets, busy with pedestrian traffic and electric streetcars.

But, as is the case with all of Austin, things have changed, and Hyde Park has become a more diversified neighborhood. With the Drag and University of Texas just below it, and hipster-ville North Loop on its north border, Hyde Park is a central Austin neighborhood that offers a tame, tree-shaded, suburban oasis for families in Austin. However, it's now a very popular place for UT students, particularly upperclassmen and graduate school students who don't want to put up with the rowdy West Campus high-rise apartment lifestyle.

Many of the original estates from the late 1800s and early 1900s remain. This a fun place to take a leisurely stroll or bike ride. Hyde Park is mostly residential, but there are a few pockets of retail spaces that offer family-friendly restaurants, an independent grocery store, and one of Austin's favorite bakeries. I'm going to walk you through some of the best foodie finds in the neighborhood.

1

GET YOUR GREEN JUICE FIX AT JUICELAND

Austin is fortunate to be home of many excellent juice companies, but JUICELAND has been the fastest growing among them. In fact, it's growing so fast, you can now find a Juiceland location at the Austin airport, and multiple shops in Dallas and Houston. What makes this juice brand so great? Probably the "Austin-ness" about it. It was started in 2001 by Matt Shook in a small cave-like nook on Barton Springs. (That location is still open, and definitely worth checking out!)

The company is built on the idea of having fun, and there's nothing more Austin-y than that! They also care about health and acceptance and gratitude and mindfulness . . . basically all of the hippy-dippy things that are easy to poke fun at, but are actually very important components of a

meaningful life. Juiceland takes great pride in their cold-pressed juices, tasty smoothies, shots, superfood lattes, and vegan food.

The drink names are pretty funny, because why use a normal smoothie name when you can use a way AWESOME name instead? The Wunder-showzen with almond milk, banana, spinach, hemp protein, and peanut butter is one of their best sellers, as is the Percolator, a tasty chocolate banana drink with caffeine from cold-brew coffee and cacao. Try the Xtra Holla Pain Yo! if you're into spicy drinks! They add jalapeño and habañero to this tasty drink. All of the fresh juices are raw and made to order, or you can grab a bottle of cold-pressed juice if you're in a hurry and want something on the run.

I'm not trying to go too healthy on you, but next up on our food crawl is another veggie-focused stop. Don't worry . . . it's absolutely delicious.

2 EAT A

VEGETARIAN MEAL AT MOTHER'S CAFE

You'll probably be greeted by a genuine "welcome, make yourself at home!" when you step into Mother's Cafe. I'm convinced that there are few restaurants full of as many gentle and caring people as a neighborhood vegetarian restaurant. MOTHER'S CAFE has been charming Austin guests

since 1980. It's labeled as a vegetarian restaurant, but you can also find tasty vegan and gluten-free options, too.

Sit down and munch on a few complimentary chips and salsa while you peruse the menu. The fun thing about a vegetarian restaurant is that it doesn't have to have a theme other than "meat-free." The menu twists and turns through various cultures and ideas. The front page has about 10 types of enchiladas, ranging from artichoke to mushroom and spinach to spicy tempeh. They're covered in homemade creamy sauces like verde, chipotle cashew, sour cream, or a dark brown mole. Top any dish with vegan cheese or sour cream if you'd prefer not to eat dairy. You can also add a generous scoop of creamy guacamole to your enchilada, which I highly recommend. Flip over the menu to find homemade carb-a-licious veggie dishes like ravioli, farfalle, and stroganoff. Mother's Cafe proves that vegetarian dishes can be hearty, comforting, and even a little sinful.

Of course, there are all the regular vegetable-focused plates like salads, stir-fries, and stuffed bell peppers. Everyone can find something tasty here.

One of my favorite things about small, independent cafes is hearing customers say to their server, "I'll have my usual!" In a culture of quick turnover in the restaurant scene and Instagrammable food trends, it's comforting to know that regulars have been dining at the same restaurant for years and years.

3

NOSH ON HOMEMADE PIES AND PASTRIES AT QUACK'S 43RD STREET BAKERY

A longtime institution in Austin, Quack's is the reincarnation of "Captain Quackenbush's Intergalactic Dessert Company and Espresso Cafe." That name is quite the mouthful! Thankfully, it was shortened to **QUACK'S 43RD STREET BAKERY** when the bakery moved to its current location in Hyde Park.

This is a neighborhood spot. Families with young students bike here on Saturday mornings, UT students walk in to get a coffee and a blueberry muffin before starting their days, and tourists are constantly walking in to try a slice of Quack's apple cinnamon pie.

The vibes are unpretentious and casual. Anyone is welcome, so you're just as likely to see a group of moms pushing strollers in as you are to see a couple meeting on a first date.

The pastry case is full of all sorts of yummy treats, and it's hard to decide what to try! The apple cinnamon pie is widely regarded as one of the best in Austin. The crust has visible layers of butter and flour, and the overflowing pie is covered in a thick, crumbly layer of butter, sugar, and spices. If it's wrong to eat the crumb topping off a pie, I don't want to be right. Grab a slice at the bakery or order a whole pie for a special occasion.

The peanut butter fudge cake is layered with thick, fluffy frosting and covered in a dense chocolate ganache. This cake is dreamy!

The Ginger Krinkle cookie is packed with spicy ginger and covered with a thick sprinkle of sugar. If ginger is your thing, you have to try this cookie.

Indulge, my friend! Then run on over to Antonelli's for the best cheese in Austin!

4

TAKE A CHEESE-TASTING CLASS AT ANTONELLI'S CHEESE

Welcome to the sweetest little place to browse and taste and shop for cheese in Austin. You can't walk into this shop and *not* smile from ear to ear.

Here's the backstory on ANTONELLI'S CHEESE. John and Kendall Antonelli got married, and on their honeymoon, John said "I'd like to open a cheese shop." *Swoon.* Most romantic conversation ever! Two years later, Antonelli's Cheese Shop opened in Hyde Park, where guests can walk in and talk to knowledgeable cheese mongers and taste the latest and greatest in the cheese world. Whether you're hosting a fancy dinner party, or just gathering to drink wine with some girlfriends on a weeknight, Antonelli's will be able to help you find the perfect cheese and accompaniments to pair with your drinks and satisfy your palate.

The small Hyde Park store is a bounty of artisanal foodie treats like honeycomb, seasonal jam, locally made chocolate bars, and fresh baguettes. There's a beautiful wine selection lining the wall. You can walk into this store empty-handed and come back out with everything you need to host an impressive backyard wine and cheese night.

John and Kendall Antonelli realized that lots of people want to learn more about cheese, so they opened their Cheese House across the street from the Cheese Shop. Curious customers can sign up for classes like "Cheese 101: The 7 Styles of Cheese" or "Holiday Pairings: How to Celebrate with Cheese!" These classes are a great date-night idea.

Another great date-night idea? A wine tasting!

5 WINE AND DINE AT VINO VINO

VINO VINO is a cozy spot to enjoy a glass of wine with a friend. The long bar on the right side of the restaurant is warm and inviting to solo patrons or small groups, and the tables scattered around the left side of the restaurant are perfect for larger groups. Hundreds of bottles of wine are displayed on wine racks attached to the wall. The bottle list boasts a fine selection of wine from around the globe; it will entice everyone, from the novice to the most advanced wino. If you're finishing a long day of food crawling and you'd like to stick to a budget, take note of the happy hour where you'll find discounts on wine by the glass and cocktails. Vino Vino manages to find the delicate balance of catering to neighborhood regulars who want to imbibe on a budget, and to wine enthusiasts who want to find something unique to drink.

The food menu is as impressive as the wine list. Vino Vino sources as locally as possible, using food from Texas French Bread (page 118), Antonelli's Cheese Shop (opposite page), and nearby farms. The cheese boards are fun if you need something to snack on with your wine. Choose three, five, or seven types of cheese, depending on the size of your group (and your hunger). And if you're looking for a grand way to end the night, the three-course prix-fixe menu allows you to choose from a selection of vegetables, seafood, meat, and dessert.

THE MUELLER CRAWL

1. Dine under the Texas sky with a meal at **CONTIGO**, 2027 ANCHOR LN., AUSTIN, (512) 614-2260, CONTIGOTEXAS.COM

2. Eat Texas-Czech pastries at **BATCH CRAFT BEER AND KOLACHES**, 3220 MANOR RD., AUSTIN, (512) 401-3025, BATCHATX.COM

3. Take time for an ice cream break at **LICK HONEST ICE CREAMS**, 1905 ALDRICH ST., SUITE 150, AUSTIN, (512) 502-5949, ILIKELICK.COM

4. Sample southern Italian cuisine at **L'OCA D'ORO**, 1900 SIMOND AVE., AUSTIN, (737) 212-1876, LOCADOROAUSTIN.COM

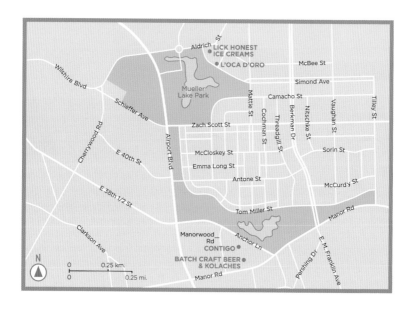

Mueller

The Shiny New Austin

FOR MOST OF THE 1900S, MUELLER WAS HOME TO AUSTIN'S MAIN airport, and . . . pretty much nothing else. When city planning officials decided to close the Robert Mueller Municipal Airport in 1999 and move it to the Bergstrom Air Force Base, Austin suddenly had a large, empty space that was primed and ready for development. In the past 20 years or so, Mueller has become home to the massive Dell Children's Medical Center, lots of public parks, plenty of retail clusters, and, of course, restaurants that cater to the thousands of young families who are buying homes in Mueller and settling down. It's no surprise, then, that the food scene in Mueller is mostly new restaurants, with a few second locations of restaurants from around town (and a reincarnated old Texas fried chicken chain). Mueller is full of kid-friendly, casual eateries. This is a place for families!

The streets of Mueller feel a bit like being in an outdoor shopping mall. Most of the retail and restaurant space is tucked into the first floor of big apartment buildings, and there are several pedestrian-only walkways where folks can wander from shop to shop. This is a lovely little village to enjoy a beautiful day of walking, shopping, and eating your way through all that Mueller has to offer.

1 DINE UNDER THE TEXAS SKY WITH A MEAL AT CONTIGO

CONTIGO has long been a favorite in Austin's restaurant scene. They call what they offer ranch-style dining, partly due to the sprawling outdoor dining area that encompasses most of the seating area. I remember brunching here when I was a student at UT with a big group of girlfriends. We'd book a big table out in the Texas sun, sip mimosas, and eat pulled pork Benedicts, fried chicken and biscuits, and big plates of beef hash while commiserating about upcoming exams. Not around for Sunday brunch? Contigo's happy hour and dinner menus are equally

impressive. The aim of Contigo is to re-create the feeling of being on the actual Contigo hunting ranch in Jim Wells County, near Corpus Christi. Grab a beer and find a picnic table; this is an exceptional place to enjoy happy hour drinks and snacks. The chicken-skin taco with chile oil, cucumber, cilantro, and camp bread is perfectly paired with a smoky Saturno cocktail of mezcal, tequila, honey, and grapefruit. Happy hour flows into dinner service, which is equally laid back. Contigo is a meat-heavy restaurant, so try the chicken liver mousse as a starter. They use smoked maple and pickles for a sweet/salty character. (Are you noticing that smoked flavors are another theme here?) Contigo's burger and fries are made on a soft, fresh challah bun; add blue cheese and bacon to take this already juicy burger to the next level. If you're dining with a crowd, try the grilled half chicken or 40-ounce bone-in rib eye, both of which serve several people. The twinkly lights that hang over the outdoor picnic tables give off a feeling of festivity. Clink those glasses and enjoy the night sky. Cheers, y'all.

2 EAT TEXAS-CZECH PASTRIES AT BATCH CRAFT BEER AND KOLACHES

Bless the family that decided to pair kolaches with craft beer, because they're a match made in heaven! **BATCH CRAFT BEER AND KOLACHES** serves some of the tastiest Czech pastries in Austin. They start with their homemade kolache dough,

which is stuffed with brisket or sausage made by the barbecue gods at Micklethwait Craft Meats, just down the road. These pillowy treats are warmed up and presented as a steaming hot meal of melty cheese, smoked meat, and spicy jalapeño. Pair that with a cold, local IPA and enjoy it with friends on one of the picnic tables on the sprawling backyard. Technically, a kolache isn't a savory thing at all. Here in the United States, we've butchered the original meaning of the word, and the pastry that's widely accepted as a kolache is actually a version of a pig in a blanket. A true Czech kolache is a sweet yeast dough, served open-face, and covered in apricots, prunes, or cherries. These authentic sweet kolaches are available at Batch as well, and they're just as exceptional as the savory options. You can stop by for breakfast and get a seasonal fruit and sweet cheese kolache, or go unconventional and try the chocolate caramel pecan. They're all fantastic!

3

TAKE TIME FOR AN ICE CREAM BREAK AT LICK HONEST ICE CREAMS

I've mentioned this before, but it bears repeating: Texas and ice cream go hand in hand. I grew up eating Blue Bell, a popular Texas grocery store brand, and my family would have no fewer than five tubs of it in our outdoor freezer on any given day. I remember walking downstairs late at night as a child to get a glass of water and seeing my dad sitting at the kitchen table, eating directly out of the half-gallon container of Moolinium Crunch to get every last little bit.

Austin has our own ice cream brands, and one of the biggest and most popular among them is LICK HONEST ICE CREAMS. Keeping true to the Austin culture, Lick cares about sourcing milk and cream from Mill-King Creamery near Waco, Texas, providing seasonal flavors and offering vegan options in their artisanal ice cream. Their Hill Country Honey and Vanilla Bean is made with local Good Flow honey, and the Mexican Plum Jam & Chocolate has thick crumbles of dark chocolate from SRSLY chocolate. I could go on and on about the ridiculously tasty flavors, but you just have to get there and try them for yourself; the proof is in the taste! The delectable flavors are true and strong. Lick only uses ingredients that are in season in Texas, so the sweet peaches you're tasting in the summer won't be available in December, when peaches don't naturally grow in Austin. Another

THE BEST-SELLING EVERYDAY FLAVORS AT LICK HONEST ICE CREAMS

Caramel Salt Lick

Texas Sheet Cake

Goat Cheese Thyme & Honey

Roasted Beets & Fresh Mint

fun thing about Lick: Regular flavors are packaged and sold in certain grocery stores, so you can try them even if you're not able to make it to a scoop shop. When I'm grocery shopping, I'll often throw a pint of Lick's Texas Sheet Cake ice cream in my grocery cart so that I can enjoy it at home, too.

4

SAMPLE SOUTHERN ITALIAN CUISINE AT L'OCA D'ORO

Let's start with the name: **L'OCA D'ORO** means "the golden goose," named after Chef Tedesco's daughter, whom he calls "Lucy Goose." This bright and beautiful Italian restaurant is all about celebrating old friends and making new ones. The pasta follows the tradition of Italy, but the ingredients are sourced

close to Austin. (There are so many restaurants in Austin that source locally! We're very fortunate to have so many exceptional farmers nearby.)

The menu features seasonal items that reflect what is freshest and most available. Since the menu is constantly changing, I can't give you exact recommendations, but talk to your server and she'll point you in the right direction.

The grilled focaccia is available year-round, and it's one of the most delicious pieces of bread I've ever put in my mouth. It's warmed over an open flame and served with cultured honey butter, so when your server brings it to your table, it will be warm, toasty, and smoked to a heavenly scent. The fresh mozzarella with kale-hazelnut pesto, colatura caramel, and Gala apples is to die for.

Pasta dishes like tagliatelle, rigatoni, gnocchi, and risotto are all there. Try the pasta tasting, which requires a full-table participation. It includes off-menu pastas with more exotic ingredients, and finishes with a giant shareable cannoli sundae for the table. L'Oca d'Oro does wine really well, so this is a great place to splurge on your bill and ask for a wine pairing to go with your pasta.

"When I first started visiting Austin 12 years ago it was all Tex-Mex and BBQ. Now there are dozens of different kinds of dining experiences available, from Tex-Mex and BBQ to refined sushi omakase, great Neapolitan pizza, and one of the best neighborhood Italian joints in America."

—Chef Fiore Tedesco,
L'Oca d'Oro

THE NORTH LOOP CRAWL

1. Brunch on farm-to-table fare at FOREIGN & DOMESTIC, 306 E. 53RD ST., AUSTIN, (512) 459-1010, FNDAUSTIN.COM

2. Play a ukulele for a free taco at TYSON'S TACOS, 4905 AIRPORT BLVD., AUSTIN, (512) 451-3326, TYSONSTACOS.COM

3. Snack on home-style Japanese food at KOMÉ, 5301 AIRPORT BLVD. #100, AUSTIN, (512) 712-5700, KOME-AUSTIN.COM

4. Eat dinner at Austin's oldest seafood counter, QUALITY SEAFOOD MARKET, 5621 AIRPORT BLVD., AUSTIN, (512) 452-3820, QUALITYSEAFOODMARKET.COM

5. Sip a well-crafted cocktail at DRINK.WELL., 207 E. 53RD ST., AUSTIN, (512) 614-6683, DRINKWELLAUSTIN.COM

6. Drink with the locals at WORKHORSE BAR, 100 E. NORTH LOOP #B, AUSTIN, (512) 553-6756, THEWHITEHORSEAUSTIN.COM

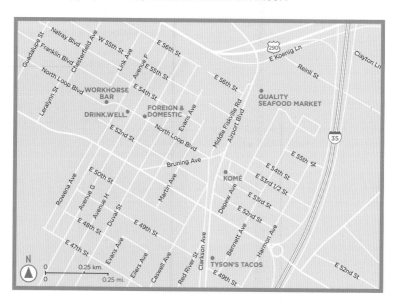

North Loop

The South Congress of North Austin

THE NORTH LOOP NEIGHBORHOOD IS CURRENTLY EXPERIENCING what South Congress went through several decades ago: It's cool. Like, really really cool. However, unlike SoCo, which has an increasing number of national brand-name stores buying out the old independent shops, North Loop is still mostly full of independent book, movie, and clothing stores, at least for the time being.

Welcome to the north Austin neighborhood where everyone wants to be. It's a little less expensive than its southern neighbor Hyde Park, and it's slightly more "Austin-y" than its eastern neighbor Mueller. Vintage clothing stores, weird car washes, hybrid coffee shop/bars, and lots of trendy restaurants provide just enough of the fun factor to turn a quiet residential neighborhood into one of the hottest places to buy a home in Austin.

While you make your way through this food crawl, embrace the grunge factor of these restaurants. This is not a sleek and polished neighborhood, like downtown Austin or Mueller. North Loop is a little rough around the edges, and we like it that way.

1

BRUNCH ON FARM-TO-TABLE FARE AT FOREIGN & DOMESTIC

You know those places you walk into and immediately get the warm fuzzies because you know everything about it is special? That's **FOREIGN & DOMESTIC.** This place was one of the first farm-to-table restaurants in Austin. They offer comforting food and warm hospitality in their teeny tiny north Austin space. How small is it? Well, the corner kitchen takes up a good 1/3 of the interior space, and an L-shaped counter wraps around the kitchen so dining customers can watch what's being prepared. The small amount of floor space that's left is full of little two- and four-top tables that can be pushed together to accommodate a group.

Chefs Sarah Heard and Nathan Lemley both come from small Texas towns, and they appreciate the food that Texas is able to provide. They source it carefully, making sure that the meat they serve is raised humanely, the crops are grown without yucky pesticides, and it's all coming from nearby, family-owned farms. From there, they use their expert touch to create gorgeous, shareable (or not!) plates that reflect the seasons. Dinner is offered five nights of the week, and a slow and lazy weekend brunch is served every Sunday morning.

The fried chicken biscuit is somewhat famous for being featured on Food Network's Diners, Drive-ins, and Dives with Guy Fieri, and if you're feeling famished, it's for you: fried chicken thigh and a sunny-side egg are placed on a warm biscuit, covered in red-eye gravy, and served with lemon confit. Another crowd favorite is the 44 Farms Steak and Eggs. 44 Farms is a family-owned cattle farm about 75 miles northeast of Austin. Since Foreign & Domestic starts with high-quality beef, you know your breakfast is going to be insanely delicious.

I once celebrated a birthday here with my husband. We sat at the counter, drank cocktails, and watched our delicious feast being prepared. It remains one of my favorite birthday meals to this day! Whether you stop by for dinner, brunch, or their daily happy hour, Foreign & Domestic will win you over.

Keep crawling for another fun North Loop breakfast spot.

2 PLAY A UKULELE FOR A FREE TACO AT TYSON'S TACOS

If you flip to the back of this book, you'll find a food crawl that's solely dedicated to breakfast tacos. But here in the North Loop food crawl, I'm also including a 24-hour taco joint that serves not just tasty breakfast tacos, but some of the best tacos in Austin, period. TYSON'S TACOS has quickly risen to fame here in ATX.

Tyson Blankemeyer realized that Austinites know a thing or two about tacos. So he moved here and learned all he could, then opened a taco shop under his own name. He calls these tacos "authentically Austin," they're actually created by Austin residents. Yep, if you eat at Tyson's Tacos often enough to rack up 300 points, you can trade them in for a menu item that you'll personally create (with Tyson) to be a permanent fixture on the menu. These tacos are crafted with love, but they're also a little weird. None of the breakfast tacos have standard names, but you can try the Avocado Abogado, filled with rib eye, egg, avocado, and skillet potato, or a Wild Feminist with egg, house sausage, potato, and pico.

If the crowd of people doesn't lure you in, the smell might. Tyson's Tacos has their own smoker in the back, and the air is full of delicious

smoky flavor. If you're stopping by for lunch or dinner, try the Burnt Ends taco. It is, as described, filled with burnt ends, onion rings, pickled jalapeños, and Valentina cream. My mouth is watering just thinking about it! If you have any hunger left at all, enjoy working your way through this endless taco menu. And if you've reached your limit, no worries! They're open 24 hours, so you can come back whenever the taco craving strikes.

Hungry for more? Komé sushi kitchen is next!

3

SNACK ON HOME-STYLE JAPANESE FOOD AT KOMÉ

This is a casual, family-style answer to all of the trendy sushi places we see so often. KOMÉ has a reasonable price point and serves Japanese comfort food, so it's no surprise that guests visit this place again, and again, and again. Husband-wife team Také and Kayo Asazu wanted to create an atmosphere that was almost like walking into someone's home to eat, so they started Komé. Rather than offering typical Japanese restaurant food, they created a menu that focuses on Japanese home-style cooking. This place serves excellent Japanese food like sushi, sashimi, bento boxes, and ramen, but rather than having a strictly authentic Japanese feel, the food also comes with little splashes of Austin and New Orleans, cities where the owners have lived. Komé is so popular, it outgrew the original location and moved into a larger building while opening a second location in downtown Austin at Fareground Food hall.

When you walk in, you'll be greeted by the entire staff saying "irrashaimasé!" which means "welcome!" in Japanese. It should put a smile on your face. The counter is a fun place to sit if you're dining solo, because you can chat with your server and watch the sushi chefs preparing your meal.

> "Many items on our menu are straight from our own dining table at home, and our own family recipes. That way, customers get to have something we actually eat every day."
>
> —Kayo Asazu,
> owner of Komé

If you're stopping by for lunch, try one of the Japanese prepared lunches. You'll be able to try miso soup, *kara-agé*, *agé-dashi* tofu, harusame noodle salad, multiple pieces of sashimi, *nigiri*, and a roll of your choice. The Sunshine Roll, made with salmon, mango, and avocado, is fun for a sweet/savory combo. Owners Také and Kayo have worked to create a menu that offers impeccable service and food, but at prices that are suitable for every day dining. (Meaning: This place won't break the bank.) The cocktails are a fun cultural twist, with fun ingredients like *genmai* syrup, *shochu*, and *matcha*. The Smokey Barrel is a strong sip of Iwai Japanese whiskey, mezcal, Thai chile syrup, Aztec chocolate bitters, orange peel, and cherries. If you're eating dinner with a crowd, order several plates of cold and hot food, and some grilled entrées. Three or four plates per person is a good place to start. Almost everything on the menu is made to be shared, family-style.

4

EAT DINNER AT AUSTIN'S OLDEST SEAFOOD COUNTER, QUALITY SEAFOOD MARKET

Right next to a busy highway, across the street from a dusty car lot, and tucked into an unimpressive brown strip mall is QUALITY SEAFOOD MARKET, the oldest seafood market and restaurant in Austin, which has been impressing its guests since 1938. Judging by the crowds that consistently gather for midweek lunches, Friday happy hours, and weekend date-night dinners, the lack of elegance is happily overlooked. Maybe the no-frills interior even adds to the charm? I'm not sure, but what I do know is that they consistently offer some of the highest quality seafood in Austin.

Quality Seafood is both a market and a restaurant. If you're looking to buy some fish to take home and cook, walk in the front door and head to the fish counter to your left, where a friendly fishmonger will tell you what's currently available. They only offer what is fresh and seasonal, so the options behind the glass are constantly changing. If you'd like to eat at the restaurant, walk up to the counter, place an order, and take a seat, and your food will be brought to you quickly. If you love oysters, you can sit at the oyster bar and watch them being shucked right in front of you. Take your pick of raw oysters from the Gulf or East Coast, or indulge in some grilled Oysters Rockefeller, all warm and buttery. The Po-Boy sandwiches are a great bet for lunch: Your choice of filling is served on a toasty, buttery hoagie with lettuce and tomato. The seafood tacos with mango pineapple pico de gallo or the hearty bowl of seafood gumbo are other delicious lunch options. If you're stopping by for a celebratory dinner, Quality Seafood has all sorts of fresh seafood entrees like Maryland-style crab cake or applewood-bacon-wrapped scallops. Sip on some frothy craft beer with your peel-and-eat shrimp, or sip on a simple house wine (remember, no frills here!) with a blackened Atlantic salmon. This might be a landlocked city, but we can still offer exceptional seafood dinners.

5

SIP A WELL-CRAFTED COCKTAIL AT DRINK.WELL.

Cozy up to your date . . . this place is a treat! **DRINK.WELL.** is the neighborhood cocktail bar and gastropub that is unapologetically itself. The small room lends itself to an intimate date night or a dark and cozy place for a group of friends to meet up. Order at the bar, then snag one of the tables scattered around the room, perch on a barstool at the counter, or linger in the limited standing room if it's especially crowded on a Saturday night.

Let's start with the homemade Twinkies, because that is, to me, the thing that makes this place incredibly special. They make them in-house every day and share the flavor on a chalk board at the side of the bar. Whatever

flavor they have when you visit, just order it. How often do you get to enjoy a homemade Twinkie?

The cocktails are inventive and fun, yet completely approachable, and the menu changes with the seasons, so you can try something different every time you show up. All of the cocktails are made with creative flavors, often using local spirits and ingredients. For instance, look at the Redbed Daisy: It's made with local Texas sotol from Desert Door Distillery in Driftwood, Texas, Linie aquavit, locally made grapefruit cordial, lemon, and habañero shrub. The last time I was here, I enjoyed the Jaded Sage, a refreshing citrusy cocktail with Laird's Straight Apple Brandy, Mizu Lemongrass Shochu, Lillet Blanc, and cardamom bitters.

The food menu is quite impressive and will remind you that Drink.well. is a gastropub in addition to being a cocktail bar. The Large Cheesemonger's Board with cheese and charcuterie from Antonelli's is a great place to start if you're feeling snacky. Drink .well.'s 44 Farms Burger & Pommes Frites is a hidden gem in the Austin dining scene. It's a simple burger with white cheddar, Bibb lettuce, tomato, and pickles, but they start with high-quality beef and serve it on their own homemade brioche bun, and the pink peppercorn aioli helps this dish to stand out as one of the superstars at Drink.well.

6

DRINK WITH THE LOCALS AT WORKHORSE BAR

Every neighborhood needs a standard dive bar where regulars can show up to see familiar faces while they enjoy a pint of beer or a well drink, and that's what WORKHORSE BAR is to the North Loop area. It's a dark, gritty bar with an Old West feel. Although it's open as early as 11 am, the tinted windows and dim lighting give it a snug and homey feel at all hours of the day or night. Walk in and find a seat at the bar, and you'll find a large tap wall that highlights local craft beer, as well as a selection of spirits for whatever cocktail strikes your fancy. The bartenders and waitstaff are friendly, and the food is served quickly. Workhorse Bar's menu offers typical bar food, but it's prepared thoughtfully with high-quality ingredients. The burgers are dense and heavy and automatically cooked to medium; if you like a little pink in your burger, be sure to ask for medium rare. They're served with your choice of cheese and placed on grilled buns, which are a little toasty but still soft enough to soak up all the juicy and drippy goodness from the burger. If you're in Austin on a warm spring evening, there's no better place to enjoy a casual drink with friends (and your dog!) than Workhorse Bar's little back patio. This is the place for people who love hole-in-the-wall restaurants; no glitz, no glam, just a lot of regulars showing up to their local bar for a relaxing evening.

THE ALLENDALE CRAWL

1. Taste baked goods galore at UPPER CRUST BAKERY, 4508 BURNET RD., AUSTIN, (512) 467-0102, UPPERCRUSTBAKERY.COM

2. Indulge in pizza and award-winning beer at PINTHOUSE PIZZA, 4729 BURNET RD., AUSTIN, (512) 436-9605, PINTHOUSEPIZZA.COM

3. Chow down on an epic lunch at NOBLE SANDWICH CO., 4805 BURNET RD., AUSTIN, (512) 666, 5124, NOBLESANDWICHES.COM

4. Step inside the most darling French-inspired cafe and grocery, ÉPICERIE, 2307 HANCOCK DR., AUSTIN, (512) 371-6840, EPICERIEAUSTIN.COM

5. Dine on interior Mexican cuisine at FONDA SAN MIGUEL, 2330 W. NORTH LOOP BLVD., AUSTIN, (512) 459-4121, FONDASANMIGUEL.COM

6. Kick off the weekend with fusion fare at THE PEACHED TORTILLA, 5520 BURNET RD., SUITE 100, AUSTIN, (512) 330-4439, THEPEACHEDTORTILLA.COM

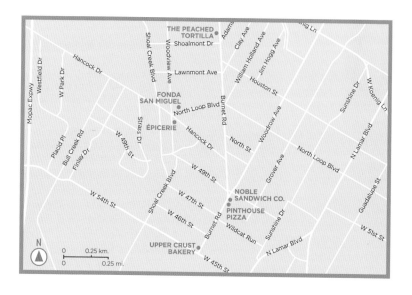

Allendale

Family-Friendly Streets and Eats

AS WE MOVE FARTHER INTO NORTH AUSTIN, THE NEIGHBORHOOD lines get a bit blurrier. Allendale, Brentwood, and Crestview were farmlands when Austin was founded in the 1800s. As the city sprawled outward from downtown, these north Austin neighborhoods became prime real estate for buyers looking for single-family homes. And of course, as houses were built, restaurants popped up as well.

One of the major north/south streets in Austin is Burnet (pronounced "burn it"). This busy street has become a major food hub in north Austin. I considered calling this chapter the "Burnet Food Crawl," but there are just too many great restaurants up here! The crawl got too long and I had to split it into two separate neighborhoods: Allendale and Crestview.

Allendale has a fun mix of ranch-style homes and midcentury modern architecture. The sprawling lots make this a desirable place to buy a home because as Austin keeps growing, Allendale seems to get closer to downtown Austin. And of course, the food scene in Allendale just keeps getting better and better.

1

TASTE BAKED GOODS GALORE AT UPPER CRUST BAKERY

If Austin, Texas, had our own version of the sitcom *Friends*, UPPER CRUST BAKERY would be the equivalent of Central Perk. It's where girlfriends gather together at big tables for weekly get-togethers, friends meet up for afternoon coffee dates, and families bring in their little ones for a Saturday morning of good eats. This is a true neighborhood gem.

The sprawling indoor space has two rooms for customers to sit and enjoy their pastries, and a large outdoor area with picnic tables for those gorgeous spring days in Austin.

I must mention the cinnamon roll first, because it's not an intuitive item to order here. Most of us want gooey cinnamon rolls with a thick, melty layer of cream cheese frosting, but Upper Crust's cinnamon roll is unconventional and has no frosting. Don't think about it too hard; just order it and enjoy devouring the whole thing. The croissant-like dough is soft and fluffy with a swirl of chewy, caramelized cinnamon and sugar throughout. I can't believe I'm saying this, but frosting would actually make this perfect cinnamon roll worse, not better.

The cakes, pies, Danishes, croissants, and other pastries in the long pastry case are all worth tasting as well. I love ordering a tall slice of apple crumble pie on the first cold day of autumn. Thick chunks of apples are piled high inside a homemade pie dough and covered with a heavy sprinkling of cinnamon and sugar and roasted pecans.

Save some room for lunch; our next stop is one of Austin's favorite pizza mini-chains!

2

INDULGE IN AWARD-WINNING BEER AT PINTHOUSE PIZZA

There's no shortage of excellent pizza in Austin, and we also have our fair share of award-winning breweries. PINTHOUSE PIZZA combines the two. This is the place to go if you love fresh, hazy, hoppy IPAs and big, chewy-crust pizzas. This is also a great place to go if you're all about eating with a crowd. The interior is full of long rows of tables and benches, so you can order a bunch of pies, a few pitchers of beer, and enjoy a big meal with all of your friends. Pinthouse's beer is a hop-lover's dream. They've long been obsessed with big, bold, hoppy profiles, but they work hard to balance them to create drinkable beers that keep customers coming back again and again. They've won medals at the fiercest beer com-petitions in the country for their IPAs and dark beers. If you're into hoppy beers, try the Man O' War, a dry-hopped IPA with 5 pounds of Citra, Simcoe, Mosaic, and Azacca hops per barrel. Looking for a dark beer? Try the Bearded Seal dry Irish stout, a bold and roasty beer with notes of coffee and dark chocolate. This beer won a gold medal at the Great American Beer Festival.

When you're ready to order a pizza, pay at the counter, take a seat, and your pizza will be deliv-ered hot and fresh to your table. The Ooh La La is a pepperoni and cheese pie covered with a pile of

fresh baby arugula, peppadew peppers, and a drizzle of spicy local honey. It's the perfect combination of spicy and sweet. And if you're a traditionalist in your pizza approach, you can't go wrong with the pepperoni and basil pizza. I've paired that with a Man O' War IPA more times than I can count, and I don't plan on stopping any time soon.

3

CHOW DOWN ON AN EPIC LUNCH AT NOBLE SANDWICH CO.

NOBLE SANDWICH CO. is the place to get massive, scrumptious sandwiches in Austin. John Bates and Brandon Martinez, the two guys who started it, took their years of experience in some of Austin's top restaurants and their passion for excellent food and funneled that into these epic eats. What's the result? Toasty sandwiches piled high with duck pastrami, pork belly, and all sorts of other delicious ingredients. They bake their own bread every day and cure the meat in-house.

True sandwich lovers will try to work through the entire menu, but if you're just here for a day and need to pick one sandwich, The Noble Pig is the sandwich that started it out. This sandwich is for pork lovers: Three types of pork (bacon, ham, and pulled pork) and melty provolone cheese are piled high on toasty bread that's been slathered in spicy mustard and mayo. The smoked duck pastrami with Russian dressing and rye pickles is worth noting, too. This is their best seller, and for good reason! One bite of this baby, and you'll be hooked. The Porkmento Burger is another crowd favorite (and a super Instagrammable sandwich, I might add!) It's an all-pork-shoulder patty covered with homemade pimento cheese, jalapeño slaw, and roasted garlic mayo. If you're in the mood for white meat, the Turkey Chop is a good place to start. Noble Pig's homemade white bread

> "The menu item I'm most proud of is our duck pastrami made into a Reuben on homemade rye; add a side of jalapeño slaw and a cold local beer."
>
> —John Bates, owner of Noble Sandwich Co.

is piled high with turkey, red onion, cucumber, and a zingy lemon coriander vinaigrette.

The sides are no joke, either. The Mac and Gouda is rich and creamy and completely customizable with tasty add-ons, like pork belly and egg, brussels sprouts, pulled pork, or bacon. The truffle fries with Parmesan are the perfect salty snack to accompany your sandwich.

I haven't even mentioned the breakfast items here, but to save time, we're going to move on to our next stop on the food crawl. Just note that The Noble Pig has an exceptional breakfast menu if you find yourself stopping by on the weekend.

4

STEP INSIDE THE MOST DARLING FRENCH-INSPIRED CAFE AND GROCERY, ÉPICERIE

ÉPICERIE is a popular brunch spot in Austin because it checks off all of the boxes: delectable French-inspired cuisine, a bright white interior a charming outdoor patio, and a sweet little grocery store where you can shop for wine, chocolate, and other delicacies. It feels a little bit like you're dining inside a neighborhood grocery store.

This is where the Austin brunch crowd loves to linger. Chef Sarah McIntosh serves classic French food in a setting that inspires rest and relaxation. Épicerie doesn't accept reservations, so pop in, order a cup of coffee, and enjoy a lazy start to your morning; there's a good chance you'll have to wait around before you can snag a table during peak brunch hours. (It will be worth the wait, though.) The croque madame, a standard item on any French menu, is a rich, indulgent start to your day with ham, *Comté*, mornay sauce, a fried egg, and crispy little *frites*. The cured salmon toast is a beautiful combination of flavors and textures: buttery bread, salty capers, creamy eggs. Whether you're stopping by for a long, lazy brunch or grabbing something to take on the go, try the pastries, like the famous beignets or the salted chocolate chip cookies. If you're visiting Austin, the cookies make great plane snacks to enjoy on your trip back home.

5

DINE ON INTERIOR MEXICAN CUISINE AT FONDA SAN MIGUEL

FONDA SAN MIGUEL is recognized as one of the best interior Mexican cuisine restaurants in the country. It's been around since 1975, so rather than being hot and trendy, this place is timeless. The walls are covered in museum-quality artwork, and bright tiles and show-stopping plants flow from room to room. This restaurant truly is one of the most stunning places to eat in Austin. Tom Gilliland and Miguel Ravago introduced authentic regional Mexican cuisine to Austin back when there were very few interior Mexican restaurants in the United States and Mexican food meant gluey enchiladas topped with yellow cheese. Fonda San Miguel has changed our approach to Mexican food. My best tip for dining here: Arrive as hungry as you can, because you'll want to taste everything.

The cocktail menu features bright and beautiful classics like mojitos and margaritas. The Silver Coin is a tequila-infused watermelon margarita, and it's sure to get the party going. The dinner menu has so many beautiful dishes, I hardly know where to start for suggestions. (Try them all!) If I must pick a few favorites, the tacos al pastor are a great place to start. One serving will give you four tacos that are full of melt-in-your-mouth pork meat and two homemade sauces. The fresh ceviches are all wonderful, as is the *queso fundido*, made with house-made pork chorizo, Swiss chard, and served with homemade tortillas. The *cochinita pibil*, a Yucatan specialty of pork baked in a banana leaf, is so exceptionally soft and flavorful, you probably won't be able to stop eating. But try to save a bit of space for *camarones en crema de chipotle* (that's "shrimp in spicy chipotle cream sauce," for anyone who's rusty on their high school Spanish language skills), or their pollo en mole poblano, a baked one-quarter chicken in the traditional mole of Puebla. As I said before: There are so many fantastic things to taste here, you'll want to arrive as hungry as possible. Enjoy every delectable morsel!

6 KICK OFF THE WEEKEND WITH FUSION FARE AT THE PEACHED TORTILLA

Do you remember back in the South Lamar chapter (page 18), when I was saying that there's a pattern of awesome Austin food trucks turning into brick-and-mortars? THE PEACHED TORTILLA is another great example of that. I'm telling you—we Austinites have mad respect for chefs who dream up a creative menu, invest in a rinky-dink little truck, and work their tails off for a few hot Texas summers and then grow enough of a crowd to expand from there. If you do all of that work, we'll support you when you open your store front.

The Peached Tortilla serves Southern food fused with the Asian flavors that Chef Eric Silverstein grew up on. This is, quite simply, food that will make almost anyone feel really happy. At its core, The Peached Tortilla pays homage to Asian street food. The menu is approachable but has a grown-up twist. For instance: Instead of serving a basic chicken wing, they make theirs with a fish sauce vinaigrette, herbs, and shallots. The Japajam Burger is a 6-ounce patty with all the stops: pepperjack cheese, fried egg, tempura onion strings, and Chinese BBQ sauce. (Psst: Be sure to snap a picture of this one to post on the 'gram before you dive in! It's a beautiful burger.) Their rendition of chow fun, the Southern Fun, is a big bowl full of delicious flavors: braised brisket, kale, bean sprouts, and wide rice noodles. Basically a party in your mouth. The Peached Tortilla is a small restaurant, but it's bright and beautiful and a lovely place to meet up with coworkers for happy hour. Whether you're stopping by for cocktails or a full-blown meal, be sure to try the instantly addicting charred brussels with bacon jam and Parmesan. You'll thank me later.

"The Austin food scene has changed dramatically in the past decade. It is night-and-day different. I remember if you wanted to eat Thai food or Italian food, you only had one or two options in town. Now you have eight to ten. It's a whole new ball game. Money is flowing in from every direction that is being used to open restaurants. If you spend a million dollars on a build out, you're no longer the exception to the rule, you are the rule. You have to adapt and keep pushing, or ultimately, you will be forgotten."

—Chef/owner
Eric Silverstein,
The Peached Tortilla

THE CRESTVIEW CRAWL

1. Dine at the ultimate neighborhood pizza and sandwich shop, **LITTLE DELI & PIZZERIA**, 7101 WOODROW AVE., SUITE A, AUSTIN, (512) 467-7302, LITTLEDELIANDPIZZA.COM

2. Take on the heat with Nashville-style chicken at **T22 CHICKEN JOINT**, 7211 BURNET RD., AUSTIN, (512) 520-1998, TUMBLE22.COM

3. Bring your pup to **YARD BAR**, 6700 BURNET RD., AUSTIN, (512) 900-3773, YARDBAR.COM

4. Celebrate nostalgia at **TOP NOTCH HAMBURGERS**, 7525 BURNET RD., AUSTIN, (512) 452-2181, TOPNOTCHAUSTIN.COM

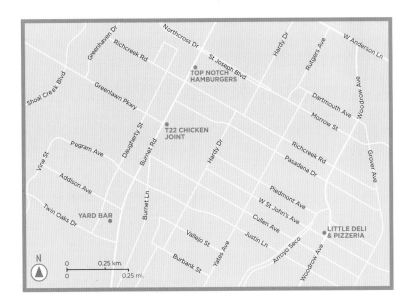

Crestview

Crawling through North Austin

IF YOU FIND YOURSELF IN FAR NORTH AUSTIN FOR THE DAY, Crestview is a cute neighborhood where you can enjoy an afternoon of strolling and eating. It was developed in the 1950s and '60s on an old dairy farm, and now it's full of bungalows with big backyards and quiet streets . . . at least for now. As the neighborhood keeps growing, more and more restaurants are choosing to open their second or third locations in Crestview. This is a fun neighborhood where residents take pride in supporting Austin businesses, so you'll find a lot of local eateries and shops.

1 DINE AT THE ULTIMATE NEIGHBORHOOD PIZZA AND SANDWICH SHOP, LITTLE DELI & PIZZERIA

LITTLE DELI & PIZZERIA is a cherished neighborhood spot for its hand-tossed New Jersey pies and massive menu of hot and cold subs. It's a true neighborhood spot, nestled right at the end of the Crestview shopping center. The lunch game is strong here, folks. Order your pizza at the counter, and the friendly staff will bring it to your table (if you're lucky enough to snag one . . . this place gets crowded at lunch!).

The thin, hand-tossed pizza is cooked on a 2-inch stone hearth, served brown and crisp yet still soft enough to fold in half. You can order a single slice for just a couple bucks if you're dining solo, or an entire pie if you're with a group. The sandwiches are made with the highest quality bread, meats, and cheeses, which are obviously a must-have for any great sandwich. This is a no-frills deli with all of the classic sandwiches you'd expect to find: BLT, turkey and swiss, meatball sub, and classic pastrami, among many others. One of their more unusual menu items is Harry's Perfect Pastrami, a big, sloppy, delicious mess of half a pound of hot top-round pastrami, Thousand Island dressing, and fresh coleslaw. It's griddled and served warm and toasty on rye bread.

Be sure to get one of the chewy chocolate cookies on your way out the door! They're baked in-house every day and taste like a mix of a rich, chewy brownie and a crisp chocolate cookie, with big chunks of walnuts interspersed in the caramelized chocolate cookie.

Hungry for more? Hot fried chicken is next!

2 TAKE ON THE HEAT WITH NASHVILLE-STYLE CHICKEN AT T22 CHICKEN JOINT

Heat lovers, get ready: **T22** fried chicken is a seriously spicy indulgence! What started as a popular food truck on West 6th Street has grown enough in popularity to open a second location: a brick-and-mortar in north Austin. T22's fried chicken is coated in Chef Harold Marmulstein's own secret blend of spices and is available in five heat levels. Start by choosing your chicken (dark, white, bone-in, mixed, or chicken tenders), and then pick a heat level:

1. Wimpy
2. Hot
3. Mo' hot!
4. Dang hot!
5. Fire in the hole!!

Once you take that first bite, there's no going back. This is for two reasons: 1) T22 fried chicken is ridiculously addicting, and 2) if you choose level 5, you might pay tomorrow. . . . Regardless of the spice level you choose, you're in for a treat with this crispy coating and moist meat. The O.G. Classic Chicken Sandwich is just that: a classic chicken sandwich without too many frills. If it ain't broke, you know? It's a simple fried chicken breast topped with kale slaw, bread and butter pickles, and Duke's mayo. Make it a Southern Chicken Sandwich by swapping the chicken breast for a thigh. The salads, sides, and desserts are all heavenly. The Hot Chicken Cobb Salad is just right when you want some greens but you also want to eat something a little bit more fun. The deviled eggs, potato salad, BBQ beans, and mac-n-cheese are the perfect accompaniments to make it into a Southern feast. Don't miss out on the pies, too. Between the Mile-High Lemon Meringue and Pecan Chocolate Toffee, you're sure to find the perfect sweet treat to wrap up your meal.

3 BRING YOUR PUP TO YARD BAR

If you find yourself in Austin with a pup who has some energy to burn, head over to **YARD BAR**, where you can set your canine loose to play and frolic in the off-leash dog park while you enjoy a pint of beer with friends! A small cover charge will let your furry friend into the safely guarded, fenced-in dog park where dozens of happy animals are chasing each other around. There are plenty of picnic tables and lawn chairs for the humans to sit and observe all the craziness. A bar with a nice selection of local and national craft beer and a variety of cocktails should fulfill all your imbibing needs. While the dog park and bar are for 21+ only, all ages are welcome at the adjacent dining patio, where you can order burgers, salads, sandwiches, and even house-made dog treats.

4

CELEBRATE NOSTALGIA AT TOP NOTCH HAMBURGERS

Alright, alright, alright . . . **TOP NOTCH HAMBURGERS** has been slinging patties since 1971 and made its claim to fame by being featured in the 1993 film *Dazed and Confused*. This is one of the few vintage drive-ins that still offers curbside service, although there's also a full dining room for guests who want to dine in. The lunch crowd is a steady stream of regulars who have been eating here for decades, as well as tourists who want to see the famous restaurant where the characters in *Dazed and Confused* stopped for food before their big night out. Top Notch's menu is pretty basic: They offer burgers, fried chicken, and a few other sandwich options. The best seller is the basic cheeseburger: a charcoal-grilled patty with mayo, cheese, tomato, lettuce,

pickles, and onions. If you're looking for something uniquely Austin, try the Longhorn Special, which comes with double meat and special sauce. The fried chicken menu is kept simple: You'll choose dark, white, or mixed meat, and add on a couple sides. Take your pick of sides from all the drive-in classics: fried onion rings, mashed potatoes and gravy, sweet buttered corn, tots, fries, or okra. There aren't a lot of frills at this restaurant, but since they've been in business since 1971, they obviously don't need them.

You don't have to Instagram your food here and tag #AustinFoodCrawls, but . . . it'd be a lot cooler if you did.

THE BARBECUE CRAWL

1. **FRANKLIN BARBECUE**, 900 E. 11TH ST., AUSTIN (512) 653-1187, FRANKLINBARBECUE.COM

2. **LA BARBECUE**, 2027 E. CESAR CHAVEZ ST., AUSTIN, (512) 605-9696, LABARBECUE.COM

3. **STILES SWITCH BBQ**, 6610 N. LAMAR BLVD., AUSTIN (512) 380-9299, STILESSWITCHBBQ.COM

4. **LEROY AND LEWIS BARBECUE**, 121 PICKLE RD., AUSTIN, (512) 945-9882, LEROYANDLEWIS.COM

5. **VALENTINA'S TEX MEX BBQ**, 11500 MANCHACA RD., AUSTIN, (512) 221-4248, VALENTINASTEXMEXBBQ.COM

6. **MICKLETHWAIT CRAFT MEATS**, 1309 ROSEWOOD AVE., AUSTIN, (512) 791-5961, CRAFTMEATSAUSTIN.COM

7. **TERRY BLACK'S BARBECUE**, 1003 BARTON SPRINGS RD., AUSTIN, (512) 394-5899, TERRYBLACKSBBQ.COM

8. **KERLIN BBQ**, 1700 E. CESAR CHAVEZ ST., AUSTIN, (512) 412-5588, KERLINBBQ.COM

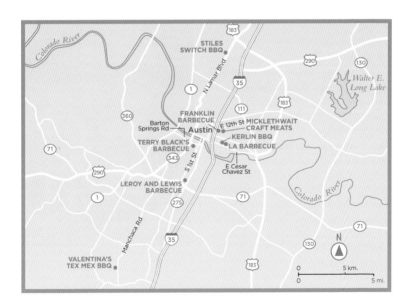

Bonus Crawl!

Barbecue

AUSTIN IS REGARDED AS ONE OF THE BEST BARBECUE CITIES IN the country, so it should be no surprise that I'm including an entire food crawl dedicated to smoked meats. At most of these barbecue joints, the meat is sold by the pound, carved right in front of the customer, and served on butcher paper. Brisket is the star of the show, but pork ribs, sausage, turkey, and all sorts of sides are typically available. I'm going to walk you through some of the best barbecue spots in Austin, from the internationally renowned giants to the little food trucks you've probably never heard of. Hope you're hungry!

1 FRANKLIN BARBECUE

Behold, the king! FRANKLIN BARBECUE, named after its founder, pitmaster Aaron Franklin, is on everyone's radar, and for good reason. The brisket is melt-in-your-mouth tender, and Franklin Barbecue has won just about every major barbecue award there is, including a James Beard Foundation Award for Best Chef: Southwest and inclusion in *Texas Monthly*'s "50 Best Barbecue Joints in the World."

2 LA BARBECUE

Like most barbecue hot spots, this one started as a little food truck. Word started spreading about the ridiculously tasty meat, and lines started forming. Eventually, they outgrew their truck and moved to the current location inside the Quickie Pickie grocery store in east Austin. Lines can be fairly long on the weekends, so stop by on a weekday if you have that option.

3 STILES SWITCH BBQ

This is an old-school Austin barbecue spot, and all of The Who's Who of the barbecue world have probably worked here at one point or another. Again, because the food is so darn tasty, the line can wrap around the building on any given day (but weekdays are typically a safe time to avoid a large crowd). All of the smoked meat by the pound is fantastic, as is their Buford T's Diablo sandwich: thick piles of brisket, spicy sausage, and jalapeños. Yum!

4

LEROY AND LEWIS BARBECUE

Say hello to the new kid on the block! Evan LeRoy and Sawyer Lewis were tired of every barbecue place serving the exact same menu (brisket, sausage, pork and beef ribs, turkey, sides, and pie), so they decided to open a "new school" barbecue truck. The menu rotates, but you can find fun things like beef cheeks, *barbacoa*-stuffed avocados, and brisket chocolate chip cookies.

> "There's no place in the world that has the concentration of great barbecue that Austin has. The level of competition is high here but that just means more delicious smoked meats for everyone! We're proud to add a unique and elevated take on traditional barbecue as well as support our local farmers and ranchers."
>
> —*Evan LeRoy, pitmaster of LeRoy and Lewis Barbecue*

5

VALENTINA'S TEX MEX BBQ

God bless the genius who decided to pair VALENTINA'S TEX MEX BBQ and barbecue, because these two food styles were meant to go together! Order from the TEX side of the menu (sliced or chopped brisket, pulled pork or chicken) or the MEX side of the menu (tacos with brisket, carnitas, pulled pollo, or beef fajita), or get some smoked meat by the pound, a pile of homemade tortillas, and make your own tacos. They're open in the mornings, too. Stop by for a giant breakfast taco full of smoked brisket, refried beans, and home-made tomato serrano salsa.

6

MICKLETHWAIT CRAFT MEATS

Tom Micklethwait founded his little bar-becue trailer in 2012, and it's already been recognized in *Texas Monthly*'s "Top 50 Barbecue Joints in Texas" and *Austin Monthly*'s "Best of ATX." You can find all the regu-lar Texas barbecue meats here, as well as some unique ones like pulled lamb, *barbacoa*, and spe-cial sausage recipes like Thai chile. The sides here are no joke, so be sure to load up on the jalapeño cheese grits, mac and cheese, and lemon poppy slaw.

7

TERRY BLACK'S BARBECUE

Twin brothers Mike and Mark Black come from a barbecue family—Black's Barbecue in Lockhart has been open since 1932. After graduating from college and working in the family restaurant, they decided to open their own smokehouse in the middle of Austin on Barton Springs Road. The long lines wrapping around the building every weekend are a clue into how obsessed Austinites have become with the melt-in-your-mouth brisket, tasty sausage links, and peppery pork ribs.

8

KERLIN BBQ

Bill Kerlin is Texas transplant by way of Arizona. After he and his wife moved to Texas and started smoking meat in the backyard, they entered (and won) some statewide barbecue competitions, which inspired them to open their own barbecue truck: Kerlin BBQ. If you haven't tried a kolache full of smoked barbecue meat, you need to try the smoked sausage, jalapeño, and cheddar kolache. Of course, the prime Angus brisket, pork ribs, and beef hot links are also exceptional.

THE BREAKFAST TACO CRAWL

1. **VERACRUZ ALL NATURAL**, 4208 MANCHACA RD., AUSTIN, VERACRUZALLNATURAL.COM

2. **FRESA'S**, 1703 S. FIRST ST., AUSTIN, (512) 992-2946, FRESASCHICKEN.COM

3. **JOE'S BAKERY & COFFEE SHOP**, 2305 E. 7TH ST., AUSTIN, (512) 472-0017, JOESBAKERY.COM

4. **POLVO'S**, 2004 S. 1ST ST., AUSTIN, (512) 441-5446, POLVOSAUSTIN.COM

5. **ROSITA'S AL PASTOR**, 1911 E. RIVERSIDE DR., AUSTIN, (512) 442-8402, ROSITASALPASTOR.COM

6. **THAI FRESH**, 909 W. MARY ST., AUSTIN, (512) 494-6436, THAI-FRESH.COM

7. **EL PRIMO**, 2011 S. 1ST ST., AUSTIN, (512) 227-5060, ELPRIMOMEX.COM

8. **CISCO'S**, 1511 E. 6TH ST., AUSTIN, (512) 478-2420, CISCOSAUSTIN.COM

9. **TACODELI**, 1500 SPYGLASS DR., AUSTIN, (512) 732-0303, TACODELI.COM

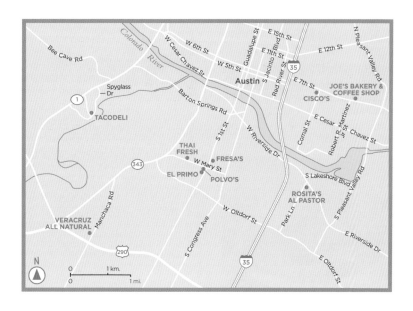

Bonus Crawl!

Breakfast Tacos

BREAKFAST TACOS ARE A RELIGION IN AUSTIN. WALK INTO A coffee shop, and you'll find breakfast tacos more easily than blueberry muffins. What make a breakfast taco so wonderful? If you're asking that, you clearly haven't tried a great one. Allow me to explain the beauty of a breakfast taco:

They're an entire meal in one hand. Similar to fast-food burgers that are designed to be eaten on the go, breakfast tacos can be consumed while walking with a beverage, like a cup of coffee, in the other hand.

They're inherently delicious. Fluffy tortillas, scrambled eggs, crispy potatoes, salty chorizo, melted cheese, and fresh, homemade salsa. It doesn't take much convincing to get someone excited about these things.

They're simple and cheap. Breakfast tacos aren't overly complicated to make, like, say, French macarons. Anyone can do it. You can make breakfast tacos at home, or you can go out to a taco stand and get a great one for about two bucks.

They can be as healthy or indulgent as you wish. Get a simple breakfast taco with organic scrambled egg whites, black beans, and a few grilled veggies if you're wanting a healthy start to the day, or go to Valentina's Tex Mex BBQ and try the Real Deal Holyfield (mesquite-smoked brisket, fried egg, potatoes, refried beans, and tomato serrano salsa) if you're vacationing and just want to live a little.

Read on to explore some of the best breakfast tacos in Austin, from the old classics to the new chains, the best taco trucks, and some fun new fusion tacos.

1

VERACRUZ ALL NATURAL

Two sisters who were raised in Veracruz, Mexico, decided to open a taco truck in Austin, and now their *migas* taco is widely regarded as the best migas taco in Austin. After the Food Network recognized their tacos as among the top five in the nation, word spread pretty quickly and VERACRUZ ALL NATURAL was able to open multiple trailers and a couple brick-and-mortars around Austin. My favorite location is the food truck parked outside Radio Coffee and Beer (page 20), because you can pair your taco with craft beer and live music. Yes, breakfast tacos are a completely acceptable choice for dinner in Austin, Texas.

2

FRESA'S

FRESA'S is worth mentioning for two reasons: First, the breakfast tacos are made on homemade flour tortillas and full of scrumptious fillings like steak and eggs, big slices of avocado, and homemade *pico de gallo*. Secondly, the location on South First Street has a beautiful outdoor creek-side patio with bright pink tables, massive live oak trees, and twinkly lights. Although you can only enjoy breakfast tacos in the morning, this is a great place to add to your list for lunch or dinner, too. Be sure to try the wood-grilled chicken, Mexican street corn, and prickly pear margaritas, and don't forget to grab a scoop of homemade ice cream on your way out.

3

JOE'S BAKERY & COFFEE SHOP

JOE'S BAKERY has been a family-run staple in Austin since 1962. They make their own tortillas, pastries, and big, hearty breakfast plates. The breakfast tacos run for just a couple dollars each, and one or two tacos should fill up the average breakfast eater. Their *carne guisada* is hearty and cozy on a cold morning, and the bacon and egg is a customer favorite on any day of the week. Locals and visitors love this place; expect crowds!

4

POLVO'S

While there are many excellent breakfast taco fillings in Austin, there are surprisingly few places that make their own homemade flour tortillas, and **POLVO'S** is one of them. (There are far more places that make their own corn tortillas.) My favorite time of day to stop in for a Polvo's breakfast taco is right when they open. There's a cook standing in the corner, flipping fresh, hot tortillas and grilling tomatoes for the homemade salsa bar. These are massive breakfast tacos with pick-your-own fillings (two are provided, and each additional one is an extra fee). Try the egg-bacon-cheese or egg-bean-potato for starters.

5

ROSITA'S AL PASTOR

If you're on the hunt for a hole-in-the-wall spot with legitimate Tex-Mex cuisine, you have to try **ROSITA'S AL PASTOR.** It's tucked into a strip mall, right between two of the most unglamorous shops (last I checked it was between a TitleMax and a dollar store), but this is where you'll find some of the best breakfast tacos in Austin. Fresh, homemade tortillas, still dusted in flour, are filled with the yummiest flavors. Don't skimp on the homemade salsa!

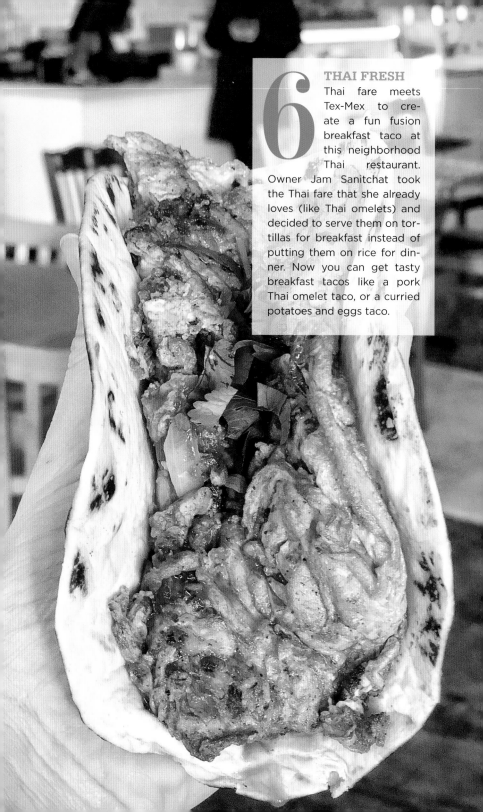

6 THAI FRESH

Thai fare meets Tex-Mex to create a fun fusion breakfast taco at this neighborhood Thai restaurant. Owner Jam Sanitchat took the Thai fare that she already loves (like Thai omelets) and decided to serve them on tortillas for breakfast instead of putting them on rice for dinner. Now you can get tasty breakfast tacos like a pork Thai omelet taco, or a curried potatoes and eggs taco.

7 EL PRIMO

If you're eager to check off a food truck and a breakfast taco in the same morning, stop by EL PRIMO for some tasty tacos at this little Mexican food truck. Go basic with the chorizo, egg, and cheese, or get some delicious *barbacoa* or *lengua* if you're feeling a bit more adventurous.

8 CISCO'S

This classic Austin bakery is named after Rudy "Cisco" Cisneros, and they've been making breakfast tacos, big plates of Mexican food, and homemade biscuits since 1950 in their iconic blue building on East 6th Street. Plenty of famous Austin politicians have eaten here; you'll see pictures of Lyndon Johnson and Bob Bullock plastered to the walls in the back room. The breakfast tacos are big and filling; start with the *migas* taco or a sausage/egg.

9 TACODELI

If you want to start a heated debate with a group of Austinites, ask them which Austin-based taco chain makes better breakfast tacos: Torchy's (Chapter 5), or TACODELI. Torchy's is by far the larger chain, with locations outside of Texas, but Tacodeli has an extremely loyal fan base, locally sourced ingredients, and new locations in big Texas cities like Houston and Dallas. Their breakfast tacos are available at any of the Austin locations, and they're also delivered to dozens of coffee shops around Austin. You won't have to look very hard to find them. The Otto is a crowd-pleaser with organic refried beans, double bacon, avocado, and jack cheese, and the Jess Special is a typical *migas* taco with loads of avocado added on top. Or just skip the menu entirely and create your own with two, three, or even four ingredients nestled inside a fresh tortilla.

THE FOOD TRUCK CRAWL

1. **SOURSOP**, 440 E. ST. ELMO RD., BLDG. G-2, AUSTIN, (512) 522-7710, SOURSOPAUSTIN.COM

2. **DEE DEE**, 2500 E. 6TH ST., AUSTIN, DEEDEEATX.COM

3. **PATRIZI'S**, 2307 MANOR RD., AUSTIN, (512) 522-4834, PATRIZIS.COM

4. **KREYOL KORNER**, 805 STARK ST., AUSTIN, (512) 596-0094, KREYOLKORNER.COM

5. **LUKE'S INSIDE OUT**, 1109 S. LAMAR BLVD., AUSTIN, (512) 589-8883, LUKESINSIDEOUT.COM

6. **GOURDOUGH'S**, 1503 S. 1ST ST., AUSTIN, (512) 912-9070, GOURDOUGHS.COM

7. **THE SOUP PEDDLER**, 501 W. MARY ST., (512) 444-7687, SOUPPEDDLER.COM

8. **BURRO CHEESE KITCHEN**, 1221 S. CONGRESS AVE., AUSTIN, (512) 865-7730, BURROCHEESEKITCHEN.COM

9. **CHURRO CO.**, 1906 S. 1ST ST., AUSTIN, (512) 905-5267, CHURROCOAUSTIN.COM

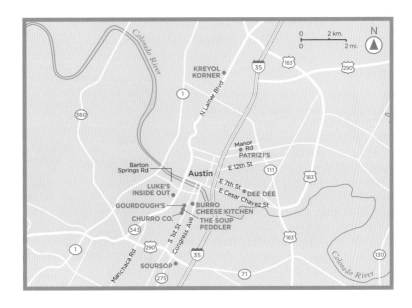

Bonus Crawl!

Food Trucks

AUSTIN'S FOOD TRUCK SCENE HAS SEEN A MASSIVE GROWTH IN the past decade. Lots of great food trucks have opened their own brick-and-mortars after a couple successful years as trucks, and others have created permanent establishments outside breweries or bars. Food trucks are a great way to enjoy lots of Austin eats on a budget. Pair up with a buddy, and share bites at as many different trucks as you can in a single day!

1

SOURSOP

SOURSOP food trailer offers pan-Asian fusion fare like Chonqing-style fried chicken with numbing Sichuan seasoning, Dippin' Tots, a spicy take on traditional Tater Tots with *togarashi*, bonito flakes, and *tsukemen* dipping broth, and the indulgent SopBurger, a feast of two fresh ground patties, *adobo* glaze, *achara* special sauce, swiss cheese, bacon fat–roasted onions, and shoestring potatoes. Hungry yet? Bonus: It's parked outside St. Elmo Brewing Co., so you can pair your food with exceptional brews from their taproom.

2 DEE DEE

DEE DEE means "good good," in Thai which makes total sense after trying a few bites of their authentic northern Thai street food. Start with the Moo Ping, two mildly sweet pork skewers with sticky rice and dipping sauce, then move on to the spicy Pad Kaprow, a spicy pork stir-fry with Thai basil, fried egg, and cucumbers before finishing it all with a sweet dessert of mango and sticky rice with coconut milk drizzled on top. Grab a sweet Thai iced coffee to take with you on the road!

3 PATRIZI'S

"Order a bunch of dishes, drink some wine, share plates, and yell at each other like a big Italian family." These are owner Nic **PATRIZI'S** words of wisdom on how to best embrace the Italian culture of eating homemade pasta at his family-owned food truck. Everything is made on-site, including the pasta (duh), tomato sauce, ricotta cheese, meatballs, pancetta, jams and jellies, infused oils, homegrown herbs, and even honey from their own beehive.

4 KREYOL KORNER

It's always island time at **KREYOL KORNER!** If you've never tried Caribbean food, you'll be pleasantly surprised by the delicious flavors prepared by Haitian-born Nahika Hillery. Start with the tropical plantain cups filled with shrimp before moving on to a combo of pork shoulder or stewed chicken, served with red beans and rice, fried sweet plantains, yuca fries, *piliz*, and sauce.

5 LUKE'S INSIDE OUT

This unassuming trailer on South Lamar serves one of the best burgers in Austin. It's pretty simple, just an 8-ounce sirloin patty served with bacon, cheddar, tomato, lettuce, onion, and love, but it's messy and delicious and everything a classic burger should be. Upgrade the chips to crinkle fries for a small charge (totally worth it), or just get a side of crinkle fries with *queso*, bacon, and jalapeños and call that a meal.

6

GOURDOUGH'S

Prepare to go into a sugar coma, my friends. **GOURDOUGH'S** Big Fat Donut's airstream trailer offers the biggest, fattest, sweetest doughnuts in town. Here are a few examples: The Fat Elvis is covered with grilled bananas and bacon, peanut butter icing, and honey, the Mother Clucker has fried chicken on top, and the Heavenly Hash is covered with marshmallow, chocolate fudge icing, and brownie bites. You'll definitely want to Instagram these babies!

7 THE SOUP PEDDLER

Although this isn't technically a food truck (there are now several brick-and-mortar locations around Austin), **THE SOUP PEDDLER** started as a man on his bike, literally peddling (and pedaling) soup to customers. The original location is a walk-up window on South 1st Street in Bouldin Creek, so it definitely has a food truck vibe. This is the place to go if you need a quick and healthy meal, like a freshly made smoothie with beet and ginger and rosewater, a raw, cold-pressed green juice, or a hot cup of homemade tomato basil soup. And although cookies are not particularly healthy, the Super Baked Cookie at The Soup Peddler is homemade with real ingredients, full of oatmeal and butter and butterscotch and topped with a sprinkling of sea salt. It is, I believe, one of the very best cookies in the entire city of Austin.

8 BURRO CHEESE KITCHEN

Melty cheese and crunchy, buttery grilled bread. Nothing better, right? **BURRO CHEESE KITCHEN** uses Easy Tiger bread (see page 36 for more about Easy Tiger) and they select only the best ingredients to make their artisan grilled cheese sandwiches. The owners of Burro Cheese Kitchen like to think of their food as a cheese plate dining experience in grilled cheese sandwich form. Everything on the menu is scrumptious, so if you're not sure where to start, try the Waylon and Willie. It's a sweet/savory sandwich of aged cheddar, Gouda, caramelized onions, peperoncini, and spicy maple bacon sauce on grilled sourdough bread.

9 CHURRO CO.

This is the perfect sweet stop to end your day of eating through Austin. **CHURRO CO.** makes their own homemade churros and offers them from traditional (tossed in cinnamon and sugar and served with chocolate, cajeta, or Nutella dipping sauce) to the most extravagant (the Campfire consists of churros tossed in graham cracker sugar, topped with Mexican chocolate sauce, whipped cream, and charred marshmallows).

"One of our favorite dishes is the Campfire, which is our rendition of the s'mores. In our minds, it's bicultural, something we strongly relate to. Growing up in the US/Mexico border, we had the opportunity of experiencing the best of both worlds. The Campfire is the mesh of the two cultures: traditional Mexican churros and the classic American campfire treat."

—David M., co-founder of Churro Co.

Appendix

Eateries by Cuisine and Specialty

American
Burro Cheese Kitchen, 201
Cafe Josie, 105
Josephine House, 103
Launderette, 74
Lenoir, 6
Mattie's, 10
Olamaie, 34
T22 Chicken Joint, 176
24 Diner, 112

Asian
Chi'Lantro BBQ, 18
Dee Dee, 197
Don Japanese Kitchen, 121
Komé, 150
Lucky Robot, 60
Peached Tortilla, The, 170
Ramen Tatsu-ya, 23
Soursop, 196
Thai Fresh, 192
Uchi, 22

Bakery
Capital City Bakery, 70
Quack's 43rd Street Bakery, 130
Sugar Mama's Bakeshop, 8
Upper Crust Bakery, 160

Bar
Ah Sing Den, 96
Drink.well., 154
Half Step, 44
Small Victory, 32
Workhorse Bar, 157
Yard Bar, 179

Barbecue
Franklin Barbecue, 184
Kerlin BBQ, 187
La Barbecue, 184
LeRoy and Lewis Barbaecue, 185

Micklethwait Craft Meats, 186
Stiles Switch BBQ, 184
Terry Black's Barbecue, 187
Valentina's Tex Mex BBQ, 186

Beer
Austin Beer Garden Brewing
    Company, 4
Banger's Sausage House and Beer
    Garden, 40
Batch Craft Beer and Kolaches, 138
Blue Owl Brewing, 78
Craft Pride, 48
Easy Tiger, 36
Lazarus Brewing Company, 88
Pinthouse Pizza, 162

Breakfast
Bouldin Creek Cafe, 2
Confituras Little Kitchen, 16
Gourdough's, 199
Juiceland, 126
Texas French Bread, 118

Burgers
Dirty Martin's Place, 120
Luke's Inside Out, 198
Top Notch Hamburgers, 180

Cafe
Cafe No Sé, 52
Counter Cafe, 110
Hillside Farmacy, 185
June's All Day, 58
Mother's Cafe, 128
Walton's Fancy and Staple, 28

Coffee
Caffè Medici, 100
Cenote, 72
Fleet Coffee, 26

Index

Photo Credits

Pg. 9 [Sugar Mama's Bakeshop, Churro Co] ©Kiera Wallner

Pg. 22 [ch2_020_uchi and ch2_021_uchi] ©Logan Crable

Pg. 26, 27 [Houndstooth] ©Houndstooth Coffee

Pg. 30, 31 [La Condesa] ©Jody Horton

Pg. 35 [ch3_016_olamaie] ©Kate LeSeuer

Pg. 34, 35 [All other Olamaie] ©Katy Fordyce

Pg. 48, 49 [Craft Pride] ©Brian Ledden

Pg. 64, 65 [Perla's] ©Casey Dunn

Pg. 75 [ch6_013_launderette] ©Marianne Lyles

Pg. 76, 77 [Bufalina] ©Nicolai McCrary

Pg. 78, 79 [Blue Owl Brewing] ©Blue Owl Brewing

Pg. 85 [Ch7_006_hillsidefarmacy] ©Mark Rodriguez

Pg. 92, 93 [Prohibition Creamery] ©Laura Aidan

Pg. 142, 143 [L'Oca d'Oro] ©L'Oca d'Oro

Pg. 166, 167 [Epicerie] ©Annie Ray

Pg. 170, 171 [ch13_019_peachedtortilla and ch13_020_peachedtortilla]
    ©Carli Rene of Inked Fingers

Pg. 201 ©Kiera Wallner